Interactions 1

Writing

4th Edition

Cheryl Pavlik

Margaret Keenan Segal

With contributions by Laurie Blass

D1518869

McGraw-Hill
Contemporary

McGraw-Hill/Contemporary

A Division of The **McGraw-Hill** Companies

Interactions 1 Writing, 4th Edition

Published by McGraw-Hill/Contemporary, a business unit of The McGraw-Hill Companies, Inc., 1221 Avenue of the Americas, New York, NY 10020. Copyright © 2002, 1996, 1990, 1985 by The McGraw-Hill Companies, Inc. All rights reserved. No part of this publication may be reproduced or distributed in any form or by any means, or stored in a database or retrieval system, without the prior written consent of The McGraw-Hill Companies, Inc., including, but not limited to, in any network or other electronic storage or transmission, or broadcast for distance learning.

Some ancillaries, including electronic and print components, may not be available to customers outside the United States.

 This book is printed on recycled, acid-free paper containing 10% postconsumer waste.

3 4 5 6 7 8 9 0 QPD/QPD 0 9 8 7 6 5 4 3 2

ISBN 0–07–246908–0
ISBN 0–07–112388–1 (ISE)

Editorial director: *Tina B. Carver*
Series editor: *Annie Sullivan*
Developmental editor: *Nancy Jordan*
Director of marketing and sales: *Thomas P. Dare*
Project manager: *Rose Koos*
Senior production supervisor: *Sandy Ludovissy*
Coordinators of freelance design: *David W. Hash/Michelle Meerdink*
Interior designer: *Michael Warrell, Design Solutions*
Senior photo research coordinator: *Carrie K. Burger*
Photo research: *Pam Carley/Sound Reach*
Supplement coordinator: *Genevieve Kelley*
Compositor: *David Corona Design*
Typeface: *10.5/12 Times Roman*
Printer: *Quebecor World Dubuque, IA*

Photo Credits
Chapter 1 Opener: © Barbara Rios/Photo Researchers, Inc.; p. 2 © Michael Newman/PhotoEdit; p. 6 © D. Young-Wolff/PhotoEdit; p. 13 © Jonathan Nourok/PhotoEdit; p. 15 © Everett Collection; Chapter 2 Opener: PhotoDisc; Chapter 3 Opener: PhotoLink/PhotoDisc; p. 35 © CAP/Corbis CD; p. 39 © Michael Newman/PhotoEdit; p. 43 © Kevin Cozad/CORBIS; p.45 © Beryl Goldberg; Chapter 4 Opener: © Robert Brenner/PhotoEdit; p.50 *(top left)* © Gale Zucker/Stock, Boston; *(top right)* © Rick Bider/PhotoEdit; *(middle)* © Robert Brenner/PhotoEdit; *(bottom)* PhotoDisc; p. 51 © Lionel Delvigne/Stock, Boston; p. 52 © John Thoeming; Chapter 5 Opener: © Jean-Claude Lejeune; p. 66 © Jean-Claude Lejeune; p. 69 © Earl & Nazima Kowall/CORBIS; Chapter 7 Opener: © Lisa M. McGeady/CORBIS; p. 92 *(top left)* © Bonnie Kamin/PhotoEdit; *(top right)* © Alan Carey/ The Image Works; *(bottom)* © Jonathan Nourok/PhotoEdit; p. 96 © CORBIS; p. 97 © Peter Menzel/Stock, Boston; p. 101 © Walter Gilardetti; p. 102 © Michael Newman/PhotoEdit; p. 104 © Walter Gilardetti; Chapter 8 Opener: © Barbara Alper/Stock, Boston; p. 108 *(all photos)* © Everett Collection; p. 109 *(both photos)* © Everett Collection; Chapter 9 Opener: © Alexander Lowry/Photo Researchers, Inc.; p. 134 © Walter Gilardetti; Chapter 10 Opener: © Rudi Von Briel/PhotoEdit; p. 140 *(top left)* © CAP/Corbis CD; *(top right)* Reuters/Bettmann Newsphotos *(bottom left)* © Spencer Grant/Photo Researchers, Inc. *(bottom right)* © Reuters New Media Inc./CORBIS; p. 144 Tony Freeman/PhotoEdit; p. 146 © Kennan Ward/CORBIS; p. 151 © CAP/Corbis CD; p. 153 © Robert Brenner/PhotoEdit; Chapter 11 Opener: © Joel Gordon; p. 160 © Joe Carini/ The Image Works; Chapter 12 Opener: © Spencer Grant/PhotoEdit

INTERNATIONAL EDITION ISBN 0–07–112388–1
Copyright © 2002. Exclusive rights by The McGraw-Hill Companies, Inc., for manufacture and export. This book cannot be re-exported from the country to which it is sold by McGraw-Hill. The International Edition is not available in North America.

www.mhcontemporary.com/interactionsmosaic

Interactions 1

Writing

Interactions 1 **Writing**

Boost your students' academic success!

Interactions Mosaic, 4ᵗʰ edition is the newly revised five-level, four-skill comprehensive ESL/EFL series designed to prepare students for academic content. The themes are integrated across proficiency levels and the levels are articulated across skill strands. The series combines communicative activities with skill-building exercises to boost students' academic success.

Interactions Mosaic, 4ᵗʰ edition features

- updated content
- five videos of authentic news broadcasts
- expansion opportunities through the Website
- new audio programs for the listening/speaking and reading books
- an appealing fresh design
- user-friendly instructor's manuals with placement tests and chapter quizzes

Exploring Ideas teaches strategies for generating writing ideas, such as brainstorming, freewriting, and interviewing.

Photos and illustrations activate prior knowledge of the topic.

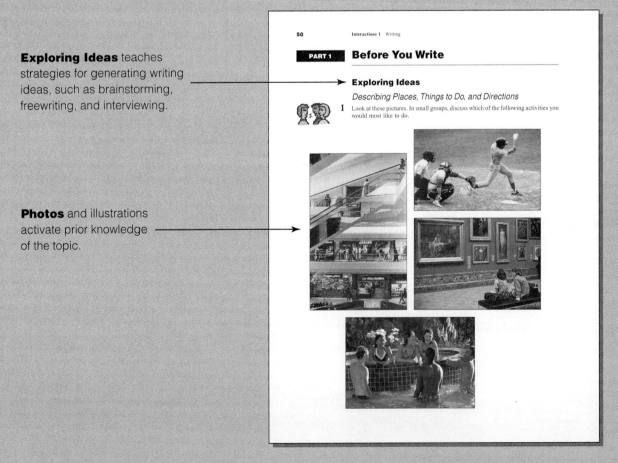

Vocabulary Building activities introduce language students may use in their writing, and develop strategies for learning vocabulary.

Organizing Ideas develops organizational skills such as outlining, writing topic sentences, and limiting the information in a paragraph.

Developing Cohesion and Style focuses on transition words, connectors, and grammatical structures that unify a paragraph.

The first page shown:

Building Vocabulary

4 How do you learn new vocabulary? One way to learn new words is to make vocabulary charts. For example, you can make a chart that lists new words by categories or topics.

What new vocabulary did you and your partner use in your interview? Work in groups of four or five. Share your words with the other members of your group. Do they have any words that you do not have? Decide which words are the most important for you and add them to the following chart. (Some words are given as examples.)

Classes	Free Time Activities	Plans	Other New Vocabulary
art	folk dancing	fashion designer	necessary
history	drawing		helpful

Organizing Ideas

Ordering Information in a Paragraph

> Information in a paragraph can be organized or ordered in different ways. For this kind of paragraph, write facts about the person you interview first. Then write the person's opinions.

Fact vs. Opinion

> When you are writing, it is important to understand the dif... and opinion. A fact is information that everyone would ag... no one would argue with it. An opinion is someone's idea. ... true. For example, *today's date* is a fact. *Paris is the capita*... *Today is an unlucky day* is an opinion. *Paris is a beautiful ci*...

The second page shown:

PART 2 **Write**

Developing Cohesion and Style

Adding Details: Adjectives

> An adjective is a word that describes a noun. Colors are adjectives. Words such as *tall, thin, curly, hungry, round, happy* and *sick* are adjectives, too. Adjectives make descriptions more interesting. They can be in two different positions:
>
> 1. After the verbs *be, seem,* and *look.*
>   **Examples**
>   The men are *young.*
>   The men look *horrified.*
>
>   *Note:* If you want to use more than one adjective you can connect them with *and*:
>   The shark is *huge and frightening.*
>
> 2. Before a noun.
>   **Example**
>   The *young* men are in a boat.

1 Look at the picture *Watson and the Shark* again. With a partner, make a list of adjectives to describe the following nouns. Use your imagination to describe the colors.

■ the boat _small, overloaded_

■ the men in the boat _____

■ the weather _____

■ the shark _____

■ the man in the water _____

■ the water _____

2 Add the adjectives from your list to the following sentences.

1. The boat is in the water. _The small, overcrowded boat is in the water._

2. There is a shark in the water. _____

3. The men are wearing clothes. _____

4. The man in the water seems _____

5. The weather looks _____ and _____

Editing Your Writing

2   Edit your paragraph using the following checklist.

Editing Checklist

1. Content
   a. Is the story clear?
   b. Is all the information important?
2. Organization
   a. Did you use time words where necessary?
   b. Did you add a title?
3. Cohesion and Style
   a. Did you vary the time words and expressions?
   b. Did you include enough description?
   c. Did you use quotations?
4. Grammar
   a. Did you use the correct forms of the past tense?
   b. Did you use the correct forms of the present continuous tense?
   c. Did you use good sentence structure (no fragments)?
5. Form
   a. Did you use commas correctly?
   b. Did you use quotation marks correctly?

Peer Editing

3   Exchange paragraphs with another student. Use editing symbols to edit each other's paragraphs. Discuss your paragraphs. Are there any other changes y...

What Do You Think?

Evaluating Folktales as Teaching Tools

Most folktales teach a lesson or moral. The real ending of this paragraph on page 87. Reread the paragraph. What does this folkta German culture in the past? What is the moral of this story? D teaches it well? Are these kinds of stories still effective in passing from generation to generation? What other things do our cultur pass down ideas?

Editing checklists equip students with a variety of tools for editing their work thoroughly.

Peer editing promotes collaboration while giving students valuable editing practice.

What Do You Think?
encourages students to relate their personal experiences to the chapter theme and to develop their critical thinking skills.

PART 4   ## A Step Beyond

Expansion Activities

1   Bring in pictures to illustrate different holidays that your class celebrates. Write captions and put the pictures on a bulletin board.

2   Make a book about holidays. Use pictures and writing to explain the holidays that you celebrate. Share your book with your classmates.

3   Write a paragraph about your favorite holiday.

4   Interview a classmate about her or his favorite holiday. In a paragraph, explain why it is her or his favorite.

Journal Writing

5   In your journal, write about how you feel about holidays now compared with how you felt when you were younger.

Focus on Testing

Organizing Your Ideas

When taking an essay exam, it is important to organize your ideas before you write. This will make your paragraph flow more smoothly. The following steps can help you organize your writing.

1. Read the topic carefully.
2. Make notes on the different points you want to write about.
3. Organize your notes. Group similar points together. Number the points (or groups of points) from the most important to the least important.
4. Check to make sure that all your points relate to the topic; delete any points that don't.
5. Write your paragraph using your organized notes.

Timed Activity: 15 Minutes

To practice this skill, choose one of the topics below. Then make notes on the topic. Finally group the ideas that belong together and decide the order that you are going to present them in.

   Being an Only Child/the Eldest/Youngest Child Is a Challenge
   The Importance of Good Nutrition
   Why I Like Living in the City (or Country)

Expansion activities encourage students to activate their writing skills in new contexts.

Journal Writing activities promote personal expression through writing.

Focus on Testing prepares students to succeed on standardized tests.

Video Activities: Online Love Story ◀

Before You Watch.   Discuss these questions in a group.

1. What is a "chat room?" Have you ever visited one?
2. Do you think the Internet is a useful way to meet new people?
3. How do you usually meet people?
4. Do you believe that there is only one man or woman in the world who is exactly "right" for each person?

Watch.   Number the following events in the order that they happened.

_____ Patrick and Vesna chatted online.

_____ They got married.

_____ Patrick came home from work late and couldn't sleep.

_____ Patrick and Vesna got engaged.

_____ Vesna came to Patrick's house.

Watch Again.   Discuss these questions in a group.

1. Patrick asked Vesna, "What do you look like?" Her answer was "You won't run from me." What did she mean?
2. Why was it easy for Patrick and Vesna to meet?
3. How soon after they met did Patrick and Vesna get engaged?
4. How soon after that did they get married?
5. What did Patrick and Vesna's friends predict about their relationship?
6. What do Patrick and Vesna say about one another?
7. What is the "Romance Network?"

After You Watch.   Work with a partner. One student is "Vesna" and the other is "Patrick." You meet in a chat room for the first time. Patrick begins by introducing himself. Then Vesna reads what he wrote and responds. Continue "chatting" until your teacher tells you to stop. You may write on paper or a computer. Be sure to ask each other questions in order to keep the conversation going.

Video news broadcasts immerse students in authentic language, complete with scaffolding and follow-up activities to reinforce writing skills.

Don't forget to check out the new *Interactions Mosaic* Website at www.mhcontemporary.com/interactionsmosaic.

■ Traditional practice and interactive activities

■ Links to student and teacher resources

■ Cultural activities

■ Focus on Testing

■ Activities from the Website are also provided on CD-ROM

Interactions 1 Writing

Grammar	Editing Skills	Critical Thinking	Test-taking Skills	Video
■ Simple past tense ■ Connecting ideas with *and, also, but,* and *so*	■ Editing for content and form	■ Fact vs. Opinion		■ Exchange Students
■ Adjectives and prepositional phrases ■ Pronouns ■ Present continuous ■ Articles *a/an, the*	■ Editing for use of adjectives and articles ■ Spelling rules for adding *-ing* to a verb	■ Comparing and contrasting		■ Winter Storm
■ Count/noncount nouns ■ Examples with *such as* ■ Appositives	■ Commas with appositives ■ Forming plural nouns ■ Spelling third-person singular verbs	■ Classifying and evaluating		■ Treat Yourself Well Campaign
■ Simple present tense ■ Future with *going to* ■ Prepositions of place, direction, and distance ■ *There* and *it*	■ Using correct form in an informal letter	■ Evaluating		■ A Homeless Shelter
■ Past tense ■ Combining sentences with time words and *because*	■ Punctuation with dependent clauses	■ Generalizing		■ Asthma and Dust Mites
■ Time clauses: *when, while,* and *as* ■ *As soon as* ■ *Then* (transitional word) ■ Quotations	■ Editing symbols	■ Evaluating		■ Chinese New Year

(continued on next page)

Interactions 1 Writing

Grammar	Editing Skills	Critical Thinking	Test-taking Skills	Video
■ Restrictive relative clauses ■ Transitional words and phrases: *in addition, for example, however* ■ Showing purpose and giving reasons with *to*	■ More editing symbols	■ Comparing and contrasting	■ Recognizing correct usage of transitional phrases	■ Marathon Man
■ Adjectives ■ Appositives ■ Historical present tense	■ Using two or more adjectives	■ Making choices	■ Summarizing	■ Quiz Shows
■ Tense review ■ *In fact* ■ Stating results with *so . . . that*	■ Long forms in formal writing ■ Spelling present and past participles ■ Capitalization	■ Evaluating	■ Managing time for an essay test	■ Online Love Story
■ Listing information with: • *In addition to, besides, another* • *The first, second, third, last* ■ Unifying a paragraph with pronouns ■ Quantifiers ■ Nonrestrictive relative clauses	■ Punctuation of nonrestrictive relative clauses	■ Examining meaning	■ Organizing ideas	■ Puerto Rican Day Parade
■ Unifying writing with synonyms and pronouns ■ Giving opinions and suggestions	■ Spelling and grammar in computer messages	■ Expressing opinions	■ Making an outline of supporting examples and reasons	■ Sight for the Blind
■ Past participles as adjectives ■ Using formal language	■ Following the format of a business letter	■ Analyzing	■ Evaluating supporting details	■ Spoiled Kids

Chapter 1

School Life Around the World

IN THIS CHAPTER

You will interview a classmate and write an article about him or her for a class newsletter. You will write the article in six steps.

PART 1

Before You Write

Exploring Ideas

Interviewing Someone

A reporter for a school newspaper is writing an article about new students on campus. He is interviewing some of the students. Look at some of his questions.

1. What is your name?
2. Where are you from?
3. What classes are you taking?
4. What do you like about this school?
5. What do you like to do in your free time?
6. What are your plans for the future?

1   You are going to interview one of the students in your class for an article for a newsletter about your class. First write some questions. Use some of the above questions and write three other questions.

2   Your teacher will write some of the questions on the board. Discuss them. Are they good questions to ask? Now look at your own questions. Are they good questions?

3   Choose the ten questions you like most. Then choose a partner and interview him or her. Write your partner's answers after the questions.

Building Vocabulary

4 How do you learn new vocabulary? One way to learn new words is to make vocabulary charts. For example, you can make a chart that lists new words by categories or topics.

What new vocabulary did you and your partner use in your interview? Work in groups of four or five. Share your words with the other members of your group. Do they have any words that you do not have? Decide which words are the most important for you and add them to the following chart. (Some words are given as examples.)

Classes	Free Time Activities	Plans	Other New Vocabulary
art	folk dancing	fashion designer	necessary
history	drawing	_____	helpful
_____	_____	_____	_____
_____	_____	_____	_____
_____	_____	_____	_____
_____	_____	_____	_____
_____	_____	_____	_____
_____	_____	_____	_____
_____	_____	_____	_____

Organizing Ideas

Ordering Information in a Paragraph

Information in a paragraph can be organized or ordered in different ways. For this paragraph, write facts about the person you interview first. Then write the person's opinions.

Fact vs. Opinion

When you are writing, it is important to understand the difference between fact and opinion. A fact is information that everyone would agree on. It is true and no one would argue with it. An opinion is someone's idea. It may or may not be true. For example, *today's date* is a fact. *Paris is the capital of France* is a fact. *Today is an unlucky day* is an opinion. *Paris is a beautiful city* is also an opinion.

5 A reporter interviewed Maria Vega for her article. After writing her notes, she numbered them in the order she wanted to write the sentences in her paragraph. Look at the reporter's questions and notes. Write F for questions about facts about Maria, O for questions about Maria's opinions, as in the example.

1. __F__ What is your name?

Maria Vega

2. _____ Where are you from?

Puerto de la Cruz, a small village in Guatemala

3. _____ How old are you?

19

4. _____ Why are you studying in Mexico?

father is Mexican, aunt lives here in Veracruz

5. _____ What classes are you taking?

English, art, history

6. _____ Why are you studying English?

necessary for work

7. _____ What do you like about Veracruz Technical College?

friendly students, helpful teachers

8. _____ What do you dislike about this college?

food in the cafeteria

9. _____ What do you do in your free time?

folk dancing, drawing

10. _____ What are your plans for the future?

international fashion designer

6 Write F or O in front of the questions that you asked in Activity 3 on page 2. Then number your questions in the order you want to write the sentences in your paragraph.

7 Show your organization to the person you interviewed. Does she or he agree with it? Does she or he want to add any information?

Writing Topic Sentences

The topic sentence tells the reader the main idea of the paragraph. It should not be too general or too specific. Don't begin paragraphs with "I am going to write about . . ." or "This paragraph is about . . ." Which of these sentences would be a good topic sentence for the paragraph about Maria Vega?

a. Maria Vega is a girl.
b. Maria Vega doesn't like the food in the cafeteria.
c. Maria Vega is one of many new students at Veracruz Technical College.

Sentence a is too general. It doesn't focus on the idea that Maria is a student. Sentence b is too specific. The whole paragraph is not about the food in the cafeteria. Sentence c is the best topic sentence. It focuses on the fact that Maria is a student and points the reader to the writer's purpose in writing about Maria— to talk about new students at the school.

8   Write a topic sentence for the paragraph you will write for the newsletter.

_____

_____

_____

PART 2   Write

Developing Cohesion and Style

Connecting Ideas

Good writers connect the ideas in their paragraphs. A paragraph with connected ideas has cohesion. Good writers also use clear and simple language. This makes their writing easy to read. A paragraph with clear and simple English has good style.

1 Look at the reporter's article below and circle the words *and, but, so,* and *also.* Which words introduce new information? Which word introduces a result? Which word introduces contrasting information?

Maria Vega is one of many new students at Veracruz Technical College. Maria is 19 and is from Puerto de la Cruz, a small village in Guatemala. She is studying here because her father is Mexican, so she wants to learn about his country. She is living in Veracruz with her aunt. Maria likes VTC very much. She likes the friendly students and the help-ful teachers. She also thinks her classes are excel-lent, but she doesn't like the food in the cafeteria. In her free time, Maria folk dances and draws. After college, she wants to be a fashion designer.

Using and *to Connect Phrases and Sentences*

When you want to say two things about a subject, use the word *and* to connect the information. Sometimes *and* connects phrases that have the same verb.

Examples

■ Maria <u>is</u> studying English. Maria <u>is</u> studying art.
  Maria Vega is studying <u>English and art</u>.

■ Yoshi <u>likes</u> reading. Yoshi <u>likes</u> watching television.
  Yoshi likes <u>reading and watching television</u>.

Sometimes *and* connects sentences that have different verbs. Use a comma before *and* when it connects two sentences.

■ Maria Vega <u>is</u> 19. Maria Vega <u>plans</u> to be a fashion designer.
  Maria Vega <u>is 19 and plans to be</u> a fashion designer.

■ Yoshi <u>works</u> in the morning. Yoshi <u>goes</u> to school at night.
  Yoshi <u>works in the morning and goes to school</u> at night.

2   Write sentences by connecting the phrases with *and.*

1. Ming Su is 26 years old.

    Ming Su comes from Taiwan.

    Ming Su is 26 years old and comes from Taiwan.

2. Amelia eats breakfast in the cafeteria.

    Amelia eats lunch in the cafeteria.

3. Reiko is 19 years old.

    Reiko likes music a lot.

4. Salma is married.

    Salma is a student.

5. Enrique likes soccer.

    Enrique plays every Saturday.

6. The school offers a good program in business.

    Its recreational facilities are excellent.

Using also *to Add Information*

When two sentences give similar ideas, you can use the word *also* in the second sentence. Find the *also* in the paragraph about Maria Vega. *Also* usually goes before the main verb in the sentence, but it goes after the verb *be.*

Examples

■ Maria Vega likes Mexico very much.
  She *also likes* the students in her school.

■ Janet is in my English class.
  She *is also* in a music class.

Use the caret symbol (^) in corrections to add something to a sentence.

Example
                                        also
  She is very pretty. She is ^very intelligent.

3   Use a ^ to add *also* to these sentences.

1.   He likes baseball. He likes rock music.

2.   Hamid is tall. He is very athletic

3.   In her free time, Maddie plays basketball. She likes to swim.

4.   Efraim works part-time. He takes care of his four children.

4   Look at your notes from the interview. Write sentences that connect similar information with *and* and *also*. Show your sentences to your partner. Are the sentences correct?

Using but *and* so *to Connect Sentences*

> You can also connect two sentences with *but* or *so*. Use a comma before these words when they connect two complete sentences.
>
> ■ *But* introduces contrasting information.
>
> **Examples**
> He thinks his English class is excellent.
> He thinks the food in the cafeteria is terrible.
> He thinks his English class is excellent, *but* he thinks the food in the cafeteria is terrible.
>
> ■ *So* introduces a result.
>
> **Examples**
> His company sells equipment to American hospitals.
> He needs English for his work.
> His company sells equipment to American hospitals, *so* he needs English for his work.

5   Connect the sentences with *and* or *but*.

1.   Alberto lives with his sister. She drives him to school every afternoon.

   _____

   _____

2.   Maria can speak English well. She needs more writing practice.

   _____

   _____

3. Western Adult School is in a beautiful location. It doesn't have very good library facilities.

_____

_____

4. Maria is Guatemalan. She is studying in Mexico.

_____

_____

6   Connect the sentences with *so* or *but*.

1. She has to work all day. She doesn't have time to do all her homework.

_____

_____

2. He likes his English class. He doesn't think the American students are very friendly.

_____

_____

3. Her company is opening an office in the United States. It needs English-speaking workers.

_____

_____

4. She likes school life. She is homesick for her family.

_____

_____

5. Pedro wants to work in Japan. He wants to learn Japanese.

_____

_____

7   Look at your notes from the interview and write two or three sentences using *and,* *but,* and *so* to connect ideas.

_____

_____

_____

_____

_____

_____

_____

Writing the First Draft

> Good writers always write and then revise their work. The first time you write is called the *first draft.* In the first draft, you put your ideas together in the form of a paragraph. When you write the first draft, think about your ideas. Don't worry too much about grammar, spelling, or form.

8   Write a paragraph about the person you interviewed. Use your organization and topic sentence from Activities 7 and 8 in Part 1. You can also use some of your sentences with *and, so, but,* and *also.* Don't worry about writing everything correctly in this first draft. You can check it and rewrite it later.

PART 3   # Edit and Revise

Editing for Content and Form

> You should edit a piece of writing at least two times.
>
> ■ The first time you edit, focus on the content of the writing: the writer's ideas, and how they are organized and connected.
> ■ The second time, focus on the form of the writing: the way the writing looks on the page, and the writer's grammar, spelling, and punctuation.

Editing Practice

1 Edit the following paragraph. Focus only on the writer's ideas and organization. Think about the following questions. Make any corrections you think are necessary.

1. Does the paragraph have a good topic sentence?
2. Are all the sentences about one subject?
3. Is the order of sentences correct?
4. Can any sentences be connected?
5. Which connecting words can you use?

A New Class Member

This is about Wichai Tongkhio. is a new member of the English composition class at Amarin Community College. There many classes at ACC. he generally likes life in Bangkok,. He likes the school. He doesn't like his dormitory. He is 18 years old. He is from a village in the north. He studying business administration, English and accounting. In his free time, he play basketball. He goes to movies. He plans to visit the United States next summer, so he needs to learn English.

---

2 Now edit the paragraph above again. This time, focus on the form. Check the writer's use of third-person singular verbs in the present tense; they should end with *-s*. Check the writer's use of negative verb forms. Check capitalization and punctuation. Finally, check the writer's sentence and paragraph form. Use the following rules to help you. Make any corrections you think are necessary. Then rewrite the paragraph using correct form.

_____

_____

_____

_____

_____

_____

_____

_____

_____

Rules for Sentence and Paragraph Form

1. Write the title in the center of the first line.
2. Capitalize all important words in the title.
3. Don't capitalize small words like *a, the, to, with,* and *at* in titles, except at the beginning of a title.
4. Skip a line between the title and the paragraph.
5. Indent (leave a space) at the beginning of every paragraph.
6. Begin every line except the first at the left margin. (Sometimes a line for the left margin is on the paper. If it isn't, leave a space of one inch.)
7. Leave a one-inch margin on the right.
8. Use a period (.) at the end of every sentence. (For rules on punctuation, see Appendix 3.)
9. Leave a small space after the period.
10. Begin every sentence with a capital letter. (For rules on capitalization, see Appendix 2.)
11. Also capitalize names of people and places. (See Appendix 2.)
12. If the last word of a line doesn't fit, use a hyphen (-) to break it. You can break a word only between syllables (**e•quip•ment**).
13. Periods and commas (,) must follow words. They can't begin a new line.
14. Every sentence in the paragraph follows the sentence before it. Start on a new line only when you begin a new paragraph.
15. In formal writing, most paragraphs have four to ten sentences. A paragraph usually has more than one or two sentences.

Editing Your Writing

3 Edit your first draft using items 1, 2, and 3 in the following checklist. Then, edit it for grammar and form using items 4 and 5.

Editing Checklist

1. Content
    a. Is the information about your partner interesting?
    b. Is it complete?
    c. Is it correct?
2. Organization
    a. Are all the sentences about one topic?
    b. Is the order of the sentences easy to follow?
3. Cohesion and Style
    a. Are your sentences clear and simple?
    b. Are they easy to understand?
    c. Can you connect any sentences?

4. Grammar
   a. Is the grammar correct?
   b. Are your verbs correct? Remember that third-person singular verbs end with -*s* in the present tense. Also check that your negative verb forms are correct.
   c. Are singular and plural nouns correct?
   d. Is the word order in your sentence correct?
5. Form
   a. Is your punctuation correct?
   b. Is your spelling correct?
   c. Are your paragraph and sentence forms correct?

Peer Editing

Everyone needs an editor. An editor looks at a writer's work and makes suggestions for changes. Even the best writers need editors because it is difficult to find mistakes in your own work.

Even though the students in your class are also learning English, they can give you helpful suggestions about your writing. They can tell you if they understand all of your ideas. They can also tell you if your ideas are in a logical order. They may know vocabulary words that you do not know. They may even be able to find errors in grammar, spelling, and punctuation.

 **4**   Show your article to the person you interviewed. Does she or he think the information in it is correct? Does she want to add anything to the paragraph? Does he think you should correct any of the grammar, spelling, punctuation, or sentence or paragraph form? If you are not sure that your classmate's suggestions are correct, check with your teacher.

Writing the Second Draft

5 Rewrite your article using correct form. Check the grammar and form one final time. Then give your article to your teacher for comments and corrections. When your teacher returns your paper, ask him or her about any comments or corrections you don't understand. The next time you write, look back at your teacher's comments. Follow your teacher's instructions, and try not to make the same mistakes again.

PART 4	# A Step Beyond

Expansion Activities

1 Share your articles with your classmates. Read them aloud or pass them around the room.

2 Make a class newsletter with your paragraphs. Type or write neat copies of the corrected paragraphs. Give the newsletter a title and share it with other English classes.

3 As a class, interview your teacher. Write possible questions on the board. You can ask her or him:

1. Where are you from?
2. What do you like to do in your free time?
3. What do you like about your job?

Think of other questions, too. Then write the paragraph together on the board. Different students can suggest different sentences. After you write all the sentences, edit the paragraph.

4 Do you know that reading automatically improves your writing? It is not important what you read—anything you enjoy reading will help you. Here are some things beginning students of English can read.

1. Special books written for beginning English language learners have easy English but adult topics. Ask your teacher if your school has any of these special readers you can borrow.
2. Books with pictures are easy to read. If you don't understand all the words, the pictures help. Comic books and children's books are excellent "picture books" for beginning students.
3. Supermarket newspapers (called *tabloids*) are fun and easy to read—just don't believe everything you find in them. They often have stories—sometimes true, sometimes not—about crazy happenings and famous people in movies, TV, and sports.

What Do You Think?

Imagine that your favorite TV, movie, or sports star (or other famous person) is experiencing a change in his or her life. Maybe she is making a new movie or starting a new TV season. Try to read something about the star (in English or your native language) in a tabloid or popular magazine. Do you think what you read is true? Why or why not?

Joan Chen, actress

Then write an article such as you might find in a tabloid about the star's new life. (Remember, it doesn't have to be true!) Where is he or she? How does he or she spend his days? What does the star like or dislike about his or her life and work? How about his or her love life? In small groups, exchange articles with your classmates. Do they think what you wrote is fact or fiction? Why?

Journal Writing

You are going to keep a journal in this class. Journals are free writing exercises: You write quickly about what you are thinking or feeling. This is for practice, so what you are saying is more important than grammar and form. Each time you write something, what you write is called an *entry.* You can buy a special notebook for your journal, or you can write entries on separate pieces of paper and keep them in a folder. Sometimes you will have a time limit, sometimes you won't.

5 For your first journal entry, write about the following topic.

1. Write for ten minutes about yourself. Write about how you are feeling, what you are doing, or what you think of your school or your English class. If you want, you can show your entry to your teacher or a classmate.

Video Activities: Exchange Students

Before You Watch.   Discuss these questions in a group.

1. Did you have exchange students in your school?
2. What are the advantages and disadvantages of studying in an overseas high school?
3. How do students celebrate graduation from high school?

Watch.   Write answers to these questions.

1. Where does Eda come from?
2. How old do you think she is?
3. Where does she live?
4. What event is Eda going to?
5. At the end of their year in the U.S., how do the visiting students feel about going back to their home countries?

Watch Again.   Read the following statements. Are the statements true or false? Write T for true, F for false.

1. _____   Brian thinks Turkish people are very different from American people.
2. _____   Eda is not homesick because she talks to her parents frequently.
3. _____   About 12 international students are studying in San Diego.
4. _____   The students are going to return to their countries in five months.
5. _____   The students are planning to meet again in the future.

After You Watch.   Imagine that you are a high school senior who has just begun a year as an exchange student in the United States. You have been in the U.S. for one week. Write a letter home. Tell about your first impressions of your host family, home, room, school, or typical day.

Chapter 2

Experiencing Nature

IN THIS CHAPTER

You will describe the painting *Watson and the Shark* by John Singleton Copley.

PART 1   # Before You Write

Exploring Ideas

1 In small groups, use these questions to discuss the painting.

1. What is the title of the painting?
2. What is a shark?
3. Which man is Watson? Why do you think he is naked?
4. How many people are in the picture?
5. What is happening in the picture?
6. How does the picture make you feel?
7. What can you see in the background? Where do you think this is happening? Why?
8. Do you think this really happened? Why or why not?
9. When do you think this scene happened?
10. Is the man going to die?

Watson and the Shark, John Singleton Copely, U.S., 1738–1815. Oil on canvas; 72 × 90 1/4 in.
(182 × 229.2 cm). Gift of Mrs. George von Lengerke Meyer. Courtesy, Museum of Fine Arts, Boston.
Reproduced with permissions. © 2000 Museum of Fine Arts, Boston. All Rights Reserved.

Building Vocabulary

2 You are going to write a paragraph describing *Watson and the Shark*. To begin, think about the vocabulary you will need to write your paragraph. The chart below lists some examples of words by parts of speech. What new vocabulary did your group use in answering the questions in Activity 1? Add your words to the chart. Find out the meaning of any words that you don't understand.

Nouns	Adjectives	Verbs	Other
rowboat	huge	reach	_____
shark	frightening	kill	_____
spear	dark	hold	_____
rope	afraid	try	_____
oar	dramatic	attack	_____
background	naked	rescue	_____
ship	_____	_____	_____
teeth	_____	_____	_____
harbor	_____	_____	_____
_____	_____	_____	_____
_____	_____	_____	_____
_____	_____	_____	_____

3 Write four sentences about the picture using as many of the vocabulary words in the list above as you can. Underline the words you used and count them. Which student in the class used the most words?

_____

_____

_____

_____

4 What do you know about sharks? Discuss what you know in small groups. Are there many sharks where you come from? Are they dangerous? What do you know about shark attacks? How many people do you think sharks kill every year? Make a note of words that may be useful for your writing.

More about Watson and the Shark

The scene in *Watson and the Shark* really happened. Mr. Brook Watson was swimming in the Havana harbor in Cuba when the shark attacked. The shark bit his leg, but Mr. Watson did not die. He was a politician, and he wanted to get publicity, so he asked the American painter John Singleton Copley (1738–1815) to paint the scene. Watson later became Lord Mayor of London.

More about Sharks

No one knows for sure where the English word *shark* comes from. Some people think it is from the Mayan Indian word *xoc,* meaning shark. Others think it is from the German *schurke,* meaning a bad person. One meaning of the English word *shark* is a dishonest person.

  People all over the world are afraid of sharks. But sharks really are not very dangerous—they only kill about 25 people every year.

Organizing Ideas

Ordering Information in a Paragraph

Descriptions often begin with general information—information that describes the whole picture. Then a writer writes specific information—information that describes smaller parts of the picture.

  The first sentence in a paragraph is often the topic sentence. In a paragraph about a work of art, it tells the name of the painting and the name of the artist. (Notice that we underline or *italicize* names of works of art.)

5 Read the following paragraph, which describes the painting below. Which sentences give general information? Which sentences give specific information?

George Seurat, French, 1859–1891, *A Sunday on La Grande Jatte,* 1848; oil on canvas, 1884–1886, 207.5 × 308 cm, Helen Birch Bartlett Memorial Collection, 1926.224. Photograph © 1994, The Art Institute of Chicago. All Rights Reserved.

A Sunday on La Grande Jatte is a picture of a park on a warm and sunny day. It seems very peaceful. In the park there are many large trees. On the left you can see a lake with some small sailboats. There are people in the park. They might be European. Some people are walking, and some are lying or sitting on the grass. Many of the people are looking at the lake. The people in the park are wearing old-fashioned clothes. The women are wearing long dresses, and some of them are carrying umbrellas. In the middle of the painting there is a small child. She is walking with her mother.

---

6 Underline the topic sentence in the paragraph.

7 Circle the adjectives in the paragraph.

8 Now look back at the painting of *Watson and the Shark.* Which of the following sentences is a good topic sentence for a paragraph about the painting?

1. *Watson and the Shark* is a good painting.
2. In this painting there are some men in a boat.
3. The men in this painting are afraid.
4. *Watson and the Shark*, by John Singleton Copley, shows a dramatic rescue.

9 Below are two general points of the painting that you should mention in your description. Can you add at least four others?

the rowboat

the sea

_____

_____

_____

_____

10 Now number the points in Activity 9 in the order that you are going to describe them.

PART 2	# Write

Developing Cohesion and Style

Adding Details: Adjectives

> An adjective is a word that describes a noun. Colors are adjectives. Words such as *tall*, *thin*, *curly*, *hungry*, *round*, *happy,* and *sick* are adjectives, too. Adjectives make descriptions more interesting. They can be in two different positions:
>
> 1. After the verbs *be*, *seem*, and *look*.
>
>   **Examples**
>   The men are *young*.
>   The men look *horrified*.
>
> *Note*: If you want to use more than one adjective you can connect them with *and*: The shark is huge *and* frightening.
>
> 2. Before a noun.
>
>   **Example**
>   The *young* men are in a boat.

1 Look at the picture *Watson and the Shark* again. With a partner, make a list of adjectives to describe the following nouns. Use your imagination to describe the colors.

■ the boat   _small, overloaded_____

■ the men in the boat _____

■ the weather _____

■ the shark _____

■ the man in the water _____

■ the water _____

2 Add the adjectives from your list to the following sentences.

1. The boat is in the water.   _The small, overcrowded boat is in the water._____

2. There is a shark in the water. _____

3. The men are wearing clothes. _____

4. The man in the water seems _____

5. The weather looks _____ and _____

Adding Details: Prepositional Phrases

Prepositions are words such as *on, in, toward, during, with*. They give information about location, direction, and time. Prepositions occur in prepositional phrases such as:

preposition	**+**	**noun**
on		the table
near		the door

Prepositions of location will be the most useful for your paragraph. Some common prepositions of location are:

on	in	at	near	under	beside	above
next to	in front of	behind	in the middle of			

Notice that prepositional phrases can be at the beginning of a sentence or at the end.

Examples

In the park there are many large trees.

There are people *in the park*.

To make your writing more interesting, put prepositional phrases in different places—not always at the beginning of a sentence.

---

3   Look at the paragraph about the Seurat painting again. Underline all the phrases that show position (location of someone or something). Most phrases that show position begin with prepositions.

4   The sentences on the next page describe the metalwork shown below in *The Tree of Life,* by the Haitian artist Georges Liautaud. Add one of the following prepositional phrases to each sentence.

- ■ at a table
- ■ to the right
- ■ out of the tree
- ■ to the left
- ■ under the tree of life
- ■ in the center

The Tree of Life by Georges Liautaud. Sculpture from the collection of Selden Rodman. Photo by Selden Rodman.

1. _In the center_ _____ is the tree of life.

2. Two children are standing _____.

3. A bird is flying _____.

4. On the right are two people sitting _____.

5. _____ a man and a woman and baby are in a boat.

6. _____ is a smaller tree.

5   Write three more sentences about *The Tree of Life* using prepositional phrases.

6   Look at the painting of *Watson and the Shark* again. Write five sentences about it using prepositions of location.

1. _There are several men in a small boat._ _____

2. _____

3. _____

4. _____

5. _____

Using Pronouns

> You can use pronouns to replace some nouns when you write a paragraph. Pronouns add variety to your writing and help to connect your ideas. However, you must make sure that it is clear what the pronouns refer to. Here are some examples of two kinds of pronouns.

	Singular	**Plural**	**Examples**	**Notes**
Subject Pronouns	I you he, she, it	we you they	*Seurat* was a French painter. He is famous today.	*He* and *him* both refer to *Seurat*.
Object Pronouns	me you him, her, it	us you them	I studied *him* in art history.	

7   Circle all the pronouns in the paragraph about Seurat's painting of the park on page 21. Then draw arrows to connect the pronouns to the nouns they represent.

8 Read the following paragraph about the painting *The Boating Party*. Change some of the nouns to pronouns. Then compare your new paragraph with a classmate's.

The painting *The Boating Party* is by Mary Cassatt. Three people are riding in a boat on the water. The painting shows only part of the boat. A woman and a child are sitting in the front of the boat. The woman is holding the child on her lap. A man is sitting in the middle of the boat. The man is rowing the boat and is facing the woman and child. The man is wearing black clothes. The woman and child are watching the man row. It is a beautiful day, and the man, woman, and child are having a good time.

Mary Cassatt.
The Boating Party,
Chester Dale
Collection, © 1995
Board of Trustees,
National Gallery of
Art, Washington,
1893–1894, oil on
canvas. 0.900 × 1.173
(35$^7/_{16}$ × 46$^1/_8$);
framed 1.21 × 1.378
(44$^1/_8$ × 54$^1/_4$).

Using Present Continuous

You can use the present continuous form of a verb to tell what is happening in a picture. Present continuous verbs have two parts:

the verb *be (is, are)* + verb + *ing*

Examples

Watson *is swimming* near the shark.
The men *are trying* to help Watson.

9 In the paragraph about *The Boating Party* on page 25, underline the present continuous forms of the verbs. You should find nine examples.

Spelling Rules for Adding –*ing* to a Verb

1. If the simple form of the verb ends in a silent -*e* after a consonant, drop the -*e* and add -*ing*.

    Examples
    race/racing   move/moving

2. If the simple form ends in -*ie*, change the -*ie* to *y* and add -*ing*.

    Examples
    die/dying   untie/untying

3. If the simple form is one syllable and ends in one consonant after one vowel, double the last consonant (except *x*) and add -*ing*.

    Examples
    run/running   get/getting
    Note that *w* and *y* at the end of words are vowels, not consonants.

4. If the simple form ends in a stressed syllable, follow the rule above for one final consonant after one vowel.

    Example
    begin/beginning
    If the last syllable is not stressed, just add -*ing*.

    Example
    happen/happening

5. In all other cases, add -*ing* to the simple form.

---

10 Write the present participles of the following verbs. Use the spelling rules above to help you.

1. swim   _swimming_   6. attack _____

2. rescue _____   7. look   _____

3. try   _____   8. bite   _____

4. throw   _____   9. see   _____

5. stand   _____   10. refer _____

Using Articles: a/an and the

A, *an*, and *the* are articles. They appear before nouns. *A* and *an* are indefinite articles. They describe general nouns. *The* is a definite article. It describes specific nouns.

	Examples	Notes
Indefinite Articles	*A:* I can drive a car, but I can't fly an airplane. *B:* Really? I can do both.	The speakers are talking about cars and airplanes in general—any cars or airplanes.
Definite Articles	*C:* Are you finished writing the reports yet? *D:* Not yet. Do you want to use the computer? *C:* That's all right. I can wait.	The speakers are talking about specific reports and a specific computer—the reports that *D* is writing and the computer that *D* is using.

Usually *a* or *an* comes before a noun when the noun appears for the first time. After that, *the* appears before the noun.

Examples	Notes
This is a painting of *an* island near Paris. *The* painting is very famous.	It is *one* painting of *one* island. It is *the* <u>specific</u> painting described in the first sentence.

11 Complete this paragraph about *The Tree of Life* with *a*, *an*, or *the*.

There is _____ large tree in the middle. Two children are standing under
_____ tree, and two children are climbing in _____ tree. _____ children
are waving. On the left is _____ man and _____ woman in _____ boat.
_____ man is fishing. _____ woman is holding _____ child. _____
large bird is flying over _____ boat. To the right is _____ smaller tree. Two
people are sitting under _____ tree at _____ table. On _____ table is
_____ plant.

Writing the First Draft

12 Write a paragraph about the painting *Watson and the Shark*. Use your notes from Activity 6 on page 24. Remember to use the present continuous to tell what is happening. Use *there is* and *there are* to name the things in the painting. Don't worry about mistakes in form and grammar. You can correct them later.

| PART 3 | # Edit and Revise |

Editing Practice

1 Edit the following paragraph for content and organization. Does it contain all of the important elements of the painting *The Starry Night?* Does the order of the description make sense? Check it also for the quality of the description. Does it make good use of adjectives? Does it describe the painting accurately?

The Starry Night is the painting by Vincent van Gogh, an Dutch artist. There are some other houses and buildings around a church. In the front of the painting are some tall, curving trees, and in the back are some rolling mountains. Our eyes follow their shapes up, around, down, and back again, like a ride on a roller coaster. In the center is a church. The stars, trees, and mountains look like they are moving. It is the beautiful scene of a sky full of bright stars.

Vincent van Gogh. *The Starry Night* (1889). Oil on canvas, 29 × 36¼". The Museum of Modern Art, New York. Acquired through the Lillie P. Bliss Bequest. Photograph © 1995 The Museum of Modern Art, New York.

2 Now edit the paragraph for form. Check it for correct use of *a/an* and *the*. Make any other changes you think are necessary. (*Hint:* There are five incorrect uses of *a/an* and *the*.)

Editing Your Writing

3 Edit your paragraph for content and organization using items 1 and 2 in the following checklist.

Editing Checklist

1. Content
   a. Are there interesting adjectives in the paragraph?
   b. Do the adjectives describe the picture well?

2. Organization
   a. Does the paragraph move from general to specific?
   b. Do you need to change the order of the sentences?

3. Cohesion and Style
   a. Can you connect any sentences?
   b. Have you used pronouns effectively?
   c. Are there appropriate descriptive adjectives?
   d. Are the prepositional phrases appropriate?

4. Grammar
   a. Are the verb forms correct? Is there an *-s* on all third-person singular verbs?
   b. Is the use of *a/an* and *the* correct?

5. Form
   Does the paragraph follow the rules for correct form? If you aren't sure, look back at the rules for sentence and paragraph form on page 12.

4 Now edit your paragraph for cohesion, style, and form using items 4 and 5 in the editing checklist.

Peer Editing

5 Show your paragraph to another student. He or she will check your work and tell you if anything is unclear.

Writing the Second Draft

6   Write the second draft of your description of *Watson and the Shark* using correct form. Check the form and grammar one more time. Then give it to your teacher for comments and corrections. When your teacher returns your paragraph, compare it with your paragraph from Chapter 1. Do you see any improvements? What problems do you still have?

What Do You Think?

Look at the different kinds of art shown below and throughout this chapter. Answer these questions.

1.   What do the Rivera mural and *Watson and the Shark* both show?
     They both show people doing things.

2.   Which two pieces of art are the most different? Why?

3.   Which two pieces of art are the most similar? Why?

4.   Which are/is old? Which is new?

5.   Which art do you like? Why?

6.   Which art don't you like? Why?

◄ Diego Rivera. *La lluvia (Rain)*. Mural, 2.05 × 2.284 m. Court of Fiestas, level 3, West Wall. Painted ca. July 1923–early 1924, Secretaria de Education Publica, Mexico City, Mexico. Schalkwijk–Art Resource, NY.

Jackson Pollock. *Number 1, 1950 (Lavender Mist)*, 1950, oil, enamel, and aluminum on canvas, 2.210 × 2.997 (87 × 118); framed: 2.235 × 3.023 × .038 (88 × 119 × 1$\frac{1}{2}$) National Gallery of Art, Washington. Ailsa Mellon Bruce Fund. ▼

| **PART 4** | # A Step Beyond |

Expansion Activities

1 Find a picture or a photo of a scene that you like, or describe a scene that you remember. First, write about the picture. What can you see in it? Are there any people there? What are they doing? Then edit your description. Have another student help you.

2 Your teacher will collect your pictures from Activity 1 and put them in the front of the room so no one knows which picture belongs to which student. Then you and your classmates will read your descriptions to the class. Guess which picture each student is describing or which description doesn't have a picture.

3 Pretend you are writing a travel brochure about a state, region, or town. Describe the place. Why should tourists visit there? What will they like? What interesting, beautiful, or historical sights are there to see? Bring in pictures if you can and make a travel brochure with your pictures and descriptions.

Journal Writing

4 Choose one of the following topics.

1. The mural *Rain* on page 30 contains writing. The writing in *Rain* says:

    Who does not feel happy
    When it begins to rain?
    It is a very sure sign
    That we shall have food.

    Discuss what this writing means. Then write for ten minutes about this saying (or you can write about another saying that you know). Is it true? Does the saying relate to your own life?

2. Describe your home. Where is it? What is in it? Do you like your home? Why or why not?

Video Activities: Winter Storm

Before You Watch.

1. The following places are mentioned in the video. Find them on a map of the United States before you watch: Washington, D.C.; New York; Ohio; New England; North Carolina.

2. Work in a group. Make a list of words to describe winter weather in a cold climate.
   Examples: snow   icy   freezing

Watch.

1. This video mainly shows a storm in the _____ part of the U.S.

   a. southern   b. western   c. northern   d. eastern

2. Which of the following words describe the weather conditions you saw in the video?
   snow   fair   storm   rain   icy   freezing   wind   warm   humid

Watch Again.   Match the places on the left with the weather conditions on the right.

Place	Weather Conditions
1. _____ Washington, D.C.	a. 12 inches of snow are expected
2. _____ New York City	b. drivers of salt trucks and snow plows didn't go to work
3. _____ New England	c. 5 inches of snow are expected
4. _____ North Carolina	d. 6 inches of snow fell
5. _____ Long Island	e. schools, businesses, and government offices closed
	f. slush

After You Watch.   Write a paragraph describing the scene. Pause the video at a scene that interests the class. Use the topic sentence below. Be sure to use adjectives and prepositional phrases in your description.

Topic Sentence: This is a picture of the United States Senate building in the snow.

Chapter 3

Living to Eat or Eating to Live?

IN THIS CHAPTER

You will write a paragraph about the special foods you eat for a holiday.

| PART 1 | # Before You Write |

Exploring Ideas

Describing Holiday Foods

1 Discuss the picture below. What are the people doing? What do you think they are eating?

2 Write in your journal about typical everyday meals that you eat. Write as much as possible in about five minutes. Don't worry about form or grammar.

3 Discuss your entry with other students. Make a list of the different kinds of food from the discussion. If you don't know the name of a food, describe it. Maybe your teacher or other students can help you.

Example

Food	Description
tacos	fried corn pancakes with meat and salad filling

4   Thanksgiving is an important American holiday. On this day, Americans give thanks for everything that they have. They eat a big meal with many special foods. Some of these foods are in the following list.

      turkey   stuffing   sweet potatoes   pumpkin pie   cranberry sauce

Think of the food you eat on a holiday. Sometimes there is no English word for a special dish. Write the word in your first language and explain it.

Your holiday: _____

Foods that you eat: _____

5   Write some sentences that compare the special food you eat on holidays with the food you eat every day.

Example   People usually prepare and eat a lot of food on Thanksgiving. The Thanksgiving meal is more delicious than our everyday meals.

_____

_____

_____

_____

_____

_____

_____

Foods from Japan

Building Vocabulary

6   Work in small groups. Look at the sentences you wrote about the special foods you eat on holidays. What vocabulary is new to you? Add your words to the following chart. Some words are in the chart as examples.

Nouns	Verbs	Adjectives	Other
celebration	celebrate	joyous	_____
feast	feast on	traditional	_____
dish	_____	typical	_____
_____	_____	_____	_____
_____	_____	_____	_____
_____	_____	_____	_____
_____	_____	_____	_____
_____	_____	_____	_____

7 Look at any of the foods that you wrote in Activities 4 and 6.

1. Which foods contain vegetables?

2. Which foods are sweet?

3. Which foods contain meat?

4. Which foods do you eat cold? hot?

Organizing Ideas

Ordering Information in a Paragraph

People often begin a paragraph with general ideas and then write more specific ones. The last sentence of a paragraph often describes a personal reaction, opinion, or feeling. For example, here are some notes about Thanksgiving:

1. Thanksgiving is a family celebration to remember the first harvest of American colonists.
2. People eat traditional foods from the first Thanksgiving feast.
3. Some typical Thanksgiving foods are turkey, stuffing, sweet potatoes, homemade bread, and pies.
4. People eat more than usual on Thanksgiving, but they feel full and happy.

8 Organize these sentences into the correct order. Number them from 1, for the first in order, to 7, for the last.

1. _____ Everyone eats more than usual, and at the end of the day we are as stuffed (full) as the turkey.

2. _____ In my family, everyone brings a special dish for the Thanksgiving meal.

3. _____ My aunt bakes a turkey and fills it with stuffing, a mixture of bread and spices.

4. __1__ Thanksgiving is a family celebration.

5. _____ They prepare many traditional foods such as turkey, sweet potatoes, and cranberry sauce.

6. _____ On this day Americans remember the first Thanksgiving feast of the early American colonists.

7. _____ My relatives also make bread, vegetables, salad, and at least four pies.

9 Make similar notes for your paragraph. Answer these questions in your notes. You may want to look back at Activities 4 and 5 on page 35.

1. What's the name of the holiday? What does it celebrate?
2. Why do people eat special dishes on this holiday?
3. What does your family eat on the holiday?
4. How do you feel about the holiday?

Writing Topic Sentences

The topic sentence

■ gives the main idea of the paragraph.

■ is always a complete sentence and has a subject and a verb.

■ is often the first sentence in a paragraph but is sometimes the second or even the last sentence.

10 Which of these main ideas about Thanksgiving are complete sentences? Write a C in front of the complete sentences.

1. __C__ The Thanksgiving meal is a special celebration.

2. _____ Thanksgiving, an important celebration.

3. _____ Families eat typical American dishes on Thanksgiving.

4. _____ A Thanksgiving feast for a family celebration.

5. _____ Thanksgiving is an important American holiday.

11 Look at the sentences about the Thanksgiving meal in Activity 8. Which sentence is the topic sentence? Underline it.

12 Look at the notes you wrote for your paragraph. First, decide if you want to add or change anything. Then write a topic sentence for your paragraph. Remember, it may be the first or second sentence in your paragraph. Exchange your notes and your topic sentence with a partner and answer these questions:

1. Is the topic sentence a complete sentence?
2. Does it give the main idea that was in your partner's notes?

PART 2

Write

Developing Cohesion and Style

Count and Noncount Nouns

There are two kinds of nouns in English: count and noncount nouns. Here are some examples.

	Examples		Notes
	Singular	*Plural*	
Count Nouns	a meal	three meals	Singular count nouns often have *a, an,* or *one* before them.
	an egg	some eggs	Plural count nouns can have numbers or expressions of
	one roll	a few rolls	quantity† before them.
	a turkey*	many turkeys	Most plural count nouns have *-s* or *-es* endings.
	a potato	potatoes	
Noncount Nouns	butter		In English, noncount nouns name things such as materials,
	juice		liquids, and qualities that do not have clear boundaries.
	turkey*		Some expressions of quantity can be used before noncount
	some salt		nouns but not *a, an,* or numbers.
	a little sugar		Noncount nouns have no plural forms.
	much food		

* Some nouns can be used as a count noun or as a noncount noun. For example:
   How many *turkeys* are you going to buy? (count)
   I love to eat *turkey* on Thanksgiving. (noncount)

† Some expressions of quantity are *some, a few, a lot of, a little, much, many.*

1 Look at the list of food items you wrote in Activity 4 on page 35. In small groups, discuss which items on your list are count nouns and which are noncount nouns. Put a ✔ after the noncount nouns. If you are not sure, look up the word in the dictionary.

Giving Examples with such as

> When you write, you can introduce examples with the phrase *such as*.
>
> **Example**
>
> On Thanksgiving Day we eat many traditional foods. The foods are turkey, sweet potatoes, and cranberries.
>
> On Thanksgiving Day we eat many traditional foods *such as* turkey, sweet potatoes, and cranberries.

2   Look at the following list of dishes from around the world. In small groups, discuss what the different dishes are. Then write the name of each dish under the correct heading as in the example.

Example

A: Who knows what ravioli is?

B: It's a kind of Italian food.

C: Right. It's a kind of small, square pasta. It's filled with cheese or meat.

- dim sum
- tacos
- samosas
- ravioli

- enchiladas
- spring rolls
- curry
- cannoli

- tamales
- mulligatawny soup
- minestrone soup
- moo shu pork

Italian	Chinese	Mexican	Indian
ravioli			

3   Now write sentences with *such as*. The first sentence is done for you.

1. Italian restaurants serve many wonderful dishes _such as ravioli, cannoli, and minestrone soup._

    _____

2. In Chinese restaurants you can try delicious dishes _____

    _____

    _____

3. _____

    _____

    _____

4. _____

    _____

    _____

4   Look at your list of nouns from Building Vocabulary on page 35. Can you use *such as* to give examples of any of the nouns? Write three sentences with *such as*. Then compare them with sentences by other students. Follow the example.

Example

On Thanksgiving Americans eat special dishes such as turkey and stuffing.

1. _____

    _____

    _____

2. _____

    _____

    _____

3. _____

    _____

    _____

Using Appositives

When you talk about typical native dishes, you sometimes have to explain what they are. You can use an appositive to explain them. An appositive is a phrase that modifies a noun and follows it directly. It is separated from the rest of the sentence by commas. If the explanation is not at the end of the sentence, another comma goes after it.

Examples

Turkey stuffing is a traditional Thanksgiving food. Stuffing is a mixture of bread and spices.

Turkey stuffing, *a mixture of bread and spices,* is a traditional Thanksgiving food.

We fill the turkey with stuffing. Stuffing is a mixture of bread and spices.

We fill the turkey with stuffing, *a mixture of bread and spices.*

5 Use appositives to combine these sentences.

1. A typical Middle Eastern dish is falafel. Falafel is a mixture of fried chick peas and spices.

   A typical Middle Eastern dish is falafel, a mixture of fried chick peas

   and spices.

2. We like to eat dim sum. Dim sum is a Chinese meal of dumplings and other small, delicious kinds of food.

   _____

   _____

3. People like to eat tempura. Tempura is a Japanese dish of fried shrimp and vegetables.

   _____

   _____

4. A favorite dish is chicken fesenjan. Chicken fesenjan is chicken in a spicy pomegranate sauce.

   _____

   _____

6 Can you explain the typical dishes for your holiday using appositives? Write four sentences with appositives. Then compare them with sentences by other students.

1. _____

   _____

2. _____

   _____

3. _____

   _____

4. _____

   _____

Writing the First Draft

7 Write your paragraph. Include the name of the holiday in your title, such as in the title "A Thanksgiving Meal." Use the topic sentence and your notes. Try to use *such as* and appositives in your paragraph.

PART 3   # Edit and Revise

Editing Practice

1 Add commas to these sentences. The first one is done for you.

1. Rijsttafel, an Indonesian rice and curry dish, is popular in Amsterdam.

2. Americans often eat hot dogs pork or beef sausages on the Fourth of July.

3. For breakfast I like to eat blintzes pancakes with a cheese filling.

4. My friend makes great bouillabaisse a French fish soup.

5. Spaghetti an Italian noodle dish is popular in North America.

6. Tacos corn pancakes with beef or chicken are everyday food in Mexico.

7. Americans often eat coleslaw a kind of cabbage salad in the summer.

8. Meat loaf a mixture of ground beef, bread crumbs and spices is an inexpensive dish.

Forming Noun Plurals

2 Write the correct plural forms of these nouns. (See Appendix 1 for spelling rules.)

1. cookie   _cookies_
2. orange   _____
3. dish   _____
4. pancake   _____
5. cherry   _____
6. peach   _____
7. tomato   _____
8. knife   _____
9. serving   _____
10. box   _____

Spelling Third-Person Singular Verbs

3   Write the correct third-person singular forms of these verbs. (See Appendix 1, pages 184 and 185, for spelling rules.)

1. He (miss)   *misses*
2. She (watch)   _____
3. He (cook)   _____
4. It (eat)   _____
5. She (hurry)   _____

6. He (mix)   _____
7. She (play)   _____
8. It (wash)   _____
9. He (drink)   _____
10. She (dry)   _____

4   Edit this paragraph twice. First, find a place to add *such as* before examples. The second time check to see if the count and noncount nouns are correct. Make any other changes you think are necessary.

Special Christmas Foods

Christmas is an important holiday for many people. People in North America prepare many special Christmas food from all over the world. Many Christmas specialties fruitcake and eggnog come from Great Britain. North Americans make fruitcakes with fruits, nuts, and liquors. Eggnog is a drink of eggs, milks, and sometimes rum. American also eat a lot of Christmas cookies. I love all the special Christmas food.

Editing Your Writing

5   Edit your paragraph using the following checklist.

Editing Checklist

1. Content
    a. Is the paragraph interesting?
    b. Is the information clear?

2. Organization
    a. Does the topic sentence give the main idea of the paragraph? Is it a complete sentence?
    b. Are all the sentences about the holiday?
    c. Are the sentences in logical order?

3. Cohesion and Style
    a. Can you connect any sentences with *and, so,* or *but*?
    b. Are the appositives correct?
    c. Does *such as* introduce examples?

4. Grammar
    a. Are the present tense verbs correct?
    b. Are the count and noncount nouns correct?

5. Form
    a. Is the paragraph form (indentation, capitalization, and punctuation) correct?
    b. Is the spelling of words with *-s* endings correct?
    c. Is the use of commas with appositives correct?

Peer Editing

6   Show your paper to another student. Does he or she understand your paragraph? Does he or she think you need to make any other corrections?

Writing the Second Draft

7 Write the second draft of your paragraph using correct form. Then give it to your teacher for comments.

8 When your teacher returns your paragraph, look at her or his comments. If you don't understand something, ask about it. Then make a list of things you do well and the things you need to work on.

What I do well:

1. _____

   _____

2. _____

   _____

3. _____

   _____

What I need to work on:

1. _____

   _____

2. _____

   _____

3. _____

   _____

What Do You Think?

Classifying Foods

Some Chinese say that there are "yang" and "yin" foods. Yang foods give people energy, and yin foods make them tired. Can you think of other ways to group food? Do you think that the food you eat can change how you act or feel? Write about what you think for ten minutes in your journal. Exchange your entries in small groups and discuss your thoughts.

PART 4   # A Step Beyond

Expansion Activities

1 Try to find pictures of the holiday celebration you described in your paragraph. Bring family pictures or pictures from books to class. In small groups, read your paragraphs aloud and show each other the pictures you have.

2 Find a classmate from another country or another part of your country, if possible. Together, choose a special occasion you both celebrate, such as a wedding or birthday. Individually write about how you each celebrate it. What do you do? What do you eat? After you write your paragraphs, exchange them. How are your celebrations the same? How are they different?

Journal Writing

3 Write in your journal for ten minutes about one or more of the following topics.

1. Why I love (or hate) holidays (or a particular holiday)
2. My favorite food
3. My favorite restaurant or café

4 Look at the recipe for apple pie. Then write a recipe for one of your favorite holiday dishes. Collect all the students' recipes. You can copy them and make a recipe booklet for each student. You could also have a party and invite everyone to bring their favorite dish.

Sifting flour

Cutting in butter with a pastry blender

Rolling out dough

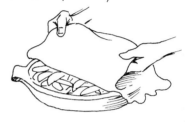
Covering pie with dough

APPLE PIE

Preheat oven to 450°F (232°C)

2 cups flour	5 to 6 cups apples
1 teaspoon salt	1/3 to 2/3 cup white or brown sugar
2/3 cup butter, margarine or shortening	1/8 teaspoon salt
1/4 cup water	1 to 1 1/2 tablespoons cornstarch
	1/4 teaspoon cinnamon
	1 1/2 tablespoons butter

Sift the flour and salt into a bowl. Then resift. Put 1/3 of this mixture into another bowl and stir in the water. Cut the butter or shortening into the flour mixture in the first bowl (use two knives or a pastry blender), until the pieces are the size of peas. Stir in the flour and water mixture and make into a ball with your hands. Roll out half and put it into a pie pan.

Peel, core and cut the apples into thin pieces. Combine the sugar, salt, cornstarch and cinnamon and mix with the apples. Put them into the pie pan with small pieces of butter. Cover the pie with the other half of the dough.

Bake in a 450°F (232°C) oven for 10 minutes. Decrease the heat to 350°F (177°C) and bake for another 35 to 50 minutes.

Adapted from *Joy of Cooking*, Irma s. Rombauer and Marion Rombauer Becker. Indianapolis: Bobbs Merrill, 1931.

Video Activities: Treat Yourself Well Campaign

Before You Watch.   Discuss these questions in a group.

1. What is the difference between "healthy" and "unhealthy" food?
2. Do you think low-fat or nonfat food can be delicious?
3. Do you like American fast food?

Watch.   Write answers to these questions.

1. What kind of food do the Wood brothers like to eat?
2. Describe some of the dishes that the tasters are eating.

Watch Again.   Complete the following statements.

1. The Wood brothers don't eat light dishes because
    a. they're more expensive than fast food
    b. they don't taste as good as "fat" food
    c. they don't care if they get fat

2. "Healthy" food contains
    a. butter   b. cream   c. vegetables   d. lots of salt

3. The pizza does <u>not</u> contain
    a. nonfat cheese   c. nonfat dressing
    b. vegetables   d. low-fat sausage

After You Watch.   Create a class cookbook. Working alone or in small groups, write a recipe for a simple, healthy dish. First make a list of ingredients. Then write directions. Follow the example on page 47. After you finish, your teacher will put all the recipes into a "book." Perhaps you can use the recipes for a class party!

Chapter 4

In the Community

IN THIS CHAPTER

You will write a letter to a friend who is coming to visit you. You will tell her or him some things you might do when she or he comes. You will also give directions to your home.

| PART 1 | # Before You Write |

Exploring Ideas

Describing Places, Things to Do, and Directions

1 Look at these pictures. In small groups, discuss which of the following activities you would most like to do.

2   Write for five minutes about your city or town. What's fun to do or see? What do you like or not like about it?

Example

> In my city, there are many theaters . . .

Building Vocabulary

3   Complete this chart with places your friend might like to visit or things she or he might like to do. Write as many places and things as you can.

Places to Visit

1. _____   4. _____
2. _____   5. _____
3. _____   6. _____

Things to Do

Inside   *Outside*

1. _____   1. _____
2. _____   2. _____
3. _____   3. _____

4   Compare your list with other students' lists. Are there any things you want to add or change?

5   Many activities use the verb *go*. Some of them are: *go sightseeing, go swimming, go fishing, go camping, go on a picnic, go to the movies.* Work with a partner. Try to think of five more activities with *go*. Then share your list with the class.

6   In your letter, you will give your friend directions to your home. Work in groups to draw a map that shows the route to each student's home. Think about these questions.

- Will your friend have to take a highway?
- If so, how will she or he get from the highway to your home?
- Are there any important landmarks (such as a lake, tall building, park, etc.) to help her or him?

Organizing Ideas

Organizing Paragraphs in a Letter

Your letter will have three paragraphs. Each paragraph has a different purpose.

■ The first paragraph will say hello, discuss the visit, and describe some of the activities you and your friend might do.

■ The second paragraph will give directions to your home.

■ The last paragraph will have only one or two sentences. The purpose of this paragraph is to say good-bye and end the letter.

---

7 Look at the following sentences. Decide if they belong in paragraph 1, 2, or 3. Write 1, 2, or 3 on the line before each sentence.

a. __1__ We can also go to a baseball game.

b. _____ There's a gas station on the corner.

c. _____ There's a concert at the City Auditorium.

d. _____ Make a left turn on Maple Avenue.

e. _____ Please write and tell me what time you will arrive.

f. _____ It won't be hard to find my house.

g. _____ It won't be easy to get theater tickets.

h. _____ I'm glad to hear that you are doing well.

i. _____ See you in two weeks.

PART 2	# Write

Developing Cohesion and Style

Selecting the Correct Verb Tense

Forms	Notes and Examples
Simple present	A repeated or habitual action in the present. **Example:** I go to the movies every Friday.
Future with *be going to*	A planned event **Example:** We're going to go to the beach tomorrow. or a prediction **Example:** She's going to fail the test.

1 Complete the sentences with the correct forms of the verbs in parentheses. Use the simple form, the present tense, or the future with *be going to*.

There _____are_____ (be) many things to do here. I'm sure that we
          1

_____ (have) a good time. It _____ (be) hot, so
          2   3

bring your bathing suit. There _____ (be) a beach very near my
                                          4

home. I _____ (know) you like music, and the London Symphony
              5

_____ (give) a concert on Saturday afternoon. That night my sister
          6

_____ (have) a birthday party. She's _____ (be)
          7   8

sixteen! On Sundays, we usually _____ (go) to a park for a picnic.
                                          9

```
BALCONY          S F ART COMMISSION
              & SAN FRANCISCO SYMPHONY
LOCATION 441832      PRESENT POPS
 305  T  21        NANCY WILSON
SEC   ROW  SEAT
920730 CE
              CIVIC AUDITORIUM
9307161822
PRICE $6.50        8:00 PM
No refunds or exchanges   No seating while performance of a work is in progress
```

Using Prepositions

Prepositions often show:

1. Place

    Examples

    The shoe store is *in* the mall.

    The concert is *at* the music hall.

    The school is *behind* the post office.

    There's a store *on* { the right. / the left. / the corner. / Main Street. }

2. Direction

    Examples

    Take Highway 6 *to* Exit 14.

    Turn right *onto* Apple Avenue.

    Drive *down* Main Street.

3. Distance

    Example

    Go straight *for* two blocks.

 **2** Underline the prepositions of place, direction, and distance in the following paragraph. Then exchange papers with another student and compare them.

Take Route 44 south <u>to</u> Exit 12. Turn right at the first light. You will be on Maple Avenue. Go straight down Maple Avenue for two miles. At the corner of Bryant and Maple you will see an elementary school. Turn right at the first street after the school. The name of the street is Roosevelt Drive. Go straight for five blocks. Then make a left turn onto Broadmoor. My apartment building isn't difficult to find. It's on the left, Number 122. You can park your car behind the building.

3   Complete the paragraph with the prepositions below. There may be more than one possible answer.

at   on   in   to   for   off

I live <u>in</u> the old part of the city. Take the number 5 bus. Get off _____

Franklin Street. You will see a large church down the street. Walk _____ the

church and turn right. Walk two blocks and turn left at _____ Smith's

Drugstore. You will be _____ Ames Avenue. Go straight _____ Ames

for two blocks. Then turn left _____ the corner of Ames and Findlay. My

house is the third one _____ the left.

4   Look at the following map. Work with a partner.

Student A
Give directions from:
the post office to the library
the elementary school to the hospital

Student B
Give directions from:
the supermarket to the park
the supermarket to the library

Exchange papers. Can you understand your partner's directions? Make any necessary corrections.

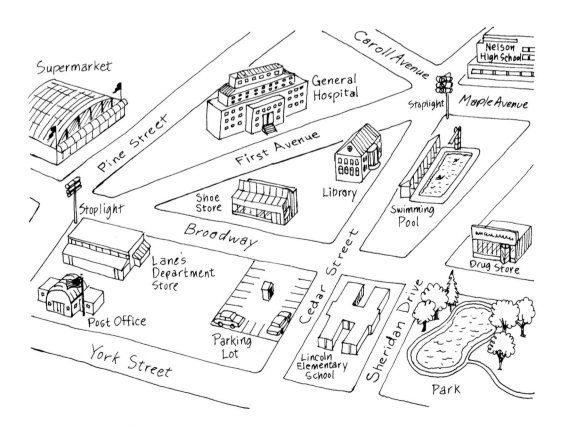

Using there *and* it

5 Sometimes the words *it* and *there* replace nouns in a sentence and sometimes they do not. Look at these sentences. Circle *it* and *there* when they replace nouns. Underline them when they don't.

1. *There* is a supermarket on the corner. *It* has a big red and white sign.

2. The museum is very interesting. I like to go *there*.

3. We can't have a picnic. *It's* raining.

4. I like New York City. *There* are beautiful parks *there*.

6 Complete the following paragraph with *there* or *it.*

__There__ are many things to see in Washington. _____ is a very
     1   2
interesting city. In the center of the city _____ is a large open area. People
                                                 3
call _____ the mall. All around the mall _____ are museums. In the
         4   5
center of the mall _____ is a very large structure. _____ is the
                        6   7
Washington Monument.

Writing the First Draft

7 Write the letter to your friend. In the first paragraph, describe what you are going to do during her or his visit. In the second paragraph, give directions to your home. In the third paragraph, say good-bye and tell your friend how excited you are about the visit.

PART 3 # Edit and Revise

Editing Practice

Using Correct Form in an Informal Letter

This is one example of an informal letter.

Date   July 12, 20XX

Dear Bill, Salutation

    I am excited about your visit. There's a lot to do here, and I'm sure we'll have a great time. On Saturday afternoon we can go to a basketball game. I think I can get tickets. In the evening we're going to go to Randy's house for dinner. After dinner we might go to a rock concert. I'm going to try to get tickets. If you want, on Sunday we can play tennis in the morning and visit the planetarium in the afternoon.

    It's easy to find my house. Just take the Connecticut Turnpike east to Exit 5. Turn left at the first light. Then you will be on Bradford Boulevard. Go straight on Bradford for three miles. Then turn left on Apple. You will see a large supermarket on your left. Go to the second light. Make a right turn on Woodgate Road. My building is on the right, three houses from the corner. It's number 417.

    See you in two weeks.

> Body

Closing {
Sincerely,

Steve

Date   The date usually appears in the upper right-hand corner. The order of the date is month, day, year. Capitalize the name of the month and put a comma after the day and before the year. Do not use a comma in the year.

Example   April 4, 20XX

Salutation   Most letters begin with *Dear*. Use the name that you usually call the person. In an informal letter a comma goes after the name.

Examples   Dear Professor Hudson,   Dear Mr. and Mrs. White,
               Dear Dr. Fitzgerald,   Dear Melinda,

Body   Indent each paragraph. In letters, paragraphs may have only one or two sentences. Although it is important to write each paragraph on a different topic, the paragraphs in a letter do not always begin with a topic sentence.

Closing   The closing of a letter begins either at the left or in the center of the page. There are many different closings. The closing that you choose depends on your relationship with the person you are writing to.

Examples   Regards,   Best wishes,   Fondly,   Love,
                 for informal letters   for letters to close friends or relatives

1   Edit this letter using the editing checklist on pages 12–13, Chapter 1. Then rewrite the letter below using correct letter form.

June 15, 20XX

Dear Mary, I'm very glad that you visit me next week. We will to have a good time. It's easy to find my house. Make left turn at the corner of Broadway and Fifth Street. Drive down Fifth two blocks. Make a right turn on Henry Street. There are a park on the corner. My house is on the left side. It are number 150. the weather is warm so we might going hiking and swimming. Please to bring your photo album. I want see the pictures of your family.

_____

_____

_____

_____

_____

_____

_____

_____

_____

_____

_____

_____

_____

_____

Addressing an Envelope

This is the correct way to address an envelope.

Return Address   Write your address in the top left-hand corner of the envelope.

Address   Write the address clearly. You may want to print it. Make sure the address is complete. If there is an apartment number, be sure to include it. It is also important to use the zip code or the postal code.

2   Address an envelope for the letter on page 58. Write your name and address as the return address. Then correct this address and write it on the envelope below.

Mary pirewali, 256 rose avenue, san jose 519478 calif united states.

Editing Your Writing

3 Edit your letter using the following checklist.

Editing Checklist

1. Content
   a. Are the activities interesting?
   b. Are the directions clear?

2. Organization
   Is each paragraph about a different topic?

3. Cohesion and Style
   a. Are the prepositions correct?
   b. Is the use of *there* and *it* correct?

4. Grammar
   Are the verb forms correct?

5. Form
   a. Is the date correct?
   b. Is the salutation correct?
   c. Do the paragraphs begin with an indentation?
   d. Is the closing in the right place?

Peer Editing

4 Exchange letters with another student. Discuss the letters. Are there any other changes you should make?

Writing the Second Draft

5 Write the second draft of your letter using correct form. Then give the letter to your teacher for comments. When your teacher returns your letter, ask him or her about any comments you don't understand. Is there any improvement in your writing?

What Do You Think?

Evaluating Community Services

Discuss the types of activities that are available at your school and in your community (sports, music, clubs, and so on). Is there a variety of activities? Are there enough activities available for people of all ages? Are there many free or inexpensive activities? What kinds of activities do you or your family do? Are there any that are not available that you would like to have?

PART 4   # A Step Beyond

Expansion Activities

1   Exchange letters with another student. Can you understand the directions? Try to draw a map from the highway to your partner's home. Then pretend you are the friend and write a reply. Thank your friend for the letter and say you are excited about going. Ask any questions you may have about the visit or the directions.

2   Write another letter to a friend who speaks English. Describe what you are doing these days. Say what you like and don't like about your life.

3   You want to invite a friend from school to your home. Write her or him an invitation note. Explain in your note how to get from school to your home. Draw a small map.

Journal Writing

4   Write for ten or fifteen minutes about one or both of these topics.

1. Compare the place you are now living with a place you lived before. Describe the places. Which one do you like best? Why?

2. Write about your community's transportation. How do people generally get around? Is the transportation good or bad?

Video Activities: A Homeless Shelter

Before You Watch.   Discuss these questions in a group.

1. Are there homeless people in your town? Tell what you know about their lives. For example, where do they get food? Where do they sleep?
2. Who should help homeless people: their families? the community? the government?
3. Why do some people become homeless?

Watch.   Discuss these questions in a group.

1. Why does Oceanside need a homeless shelter?
2. What does the proposed shelter look like?
3. What is the woman in the hat trying to do?

Watch Again.   Fill in the blanks.

1. There are _____ homeless people in Oceanside.

2. However, now there are only _____ shelter beds.

3. The Oceanside City Council will give _____ dollars for the new shelter.

4. The new shelter will have _____ beds.

5. The new shelter will be for single men and women and couples. Families will stay in _____.

6. The city needs to raise money, and it is also asking people in the community to _____.

After You Watch.   Write a letter to your family and friends. Ask them to donate money for a new homeless shelter in your town. In your letter,

■ tell people why you are writing
■ explain the problem—why the town needs a new shelter
■ ask people to give money
■ thank them for helping

You can start your letter like this:

Dear Family and Friends,
I am writing to ask for your help. We have a serious problem
in our town . . .

Chapter 5

Home

IN THIS CHAPTER

You will write a paragraph about a part of your life.

PART 1

Before You Write

Exploring Ideas

Using a Lifeline

1 Draw a line down the middle of a piece of paper. The top of the line represents the year you were born, and the bottom of the line is the present time. You can write some ages along the line too, as in the picture below. Think about your life and write some of the important events on the left of the lifeline. Write your feelings about your life on the right. Write in English if possible, but don't worry about correctness. If you can't think of something in English, use your native language. You can use pictures and symbols, and you may also want to look at family photographs. Look at the woman's lifeline on page 65 as an example.

Building Vocabulary

2 Did you need to write any words or phrases in your native language? Look them up in a dictionary and write their meanings in English. Then write a sentence that uses each new word or phrase. Show your sentences to the other students in your group. Do they think you used the words correctly? Ask your teacher to check your sentences.

3 Show your lifeline to some other students and talk about your life. Ask each other questions. What do the other students think is interesting about your life?

Organizing Ideas

Limiting Information

You can't write about your whole life in one paragraph, so you need to choose one part of your life to write about. You may want to write about your childhood, your school years, or one important event in your life.

4   Look at the woman's lifeline again. Discuss where a paragraph on a part of her life can begin and end.

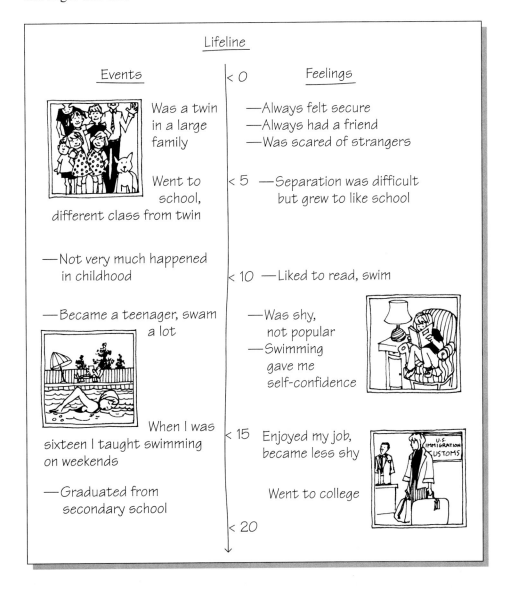

Lifeline

Events		Feelings

Events   < 0   Feelings

Was a twin in a large family

—Always felt secure
—Always had a friend
—Was scared of strangers

Went to school, different class from twin

< 5 —Separation was difficult but grew to like school

—Not very much happened in childhood

< 10 —Liked to read, swim

—Became a teenager, swam a lot

—Was shy, not popular
—Swimming gave me self-confidence

When I was sixteen I taught swimming on weekends

< 15 Enjoyed my job, became less shy

—Graduated from secondary school

Went to college

< 20

5 Now look at your own lifeline and choose a part of your life to write about. As you think about the different parts, consider the following points.

■ Is this part of my life interesting? Often unusual or funny events are more interesting to write about.

■ Is this part of my life important?

■ Is this part of my life about one topic? Don't try to write about too many events or times. Everything in your paragraph should be about one main subject.

Discuss your decision with some classmates. Do they agree with your choice?

Making Paragraph Notes

6 Look at the part of the lifeline you chose and add information you think is important. Cross out information that is not about the topic of your paragraph.

Writing Topic Sentences

7 Look at these paragraph notes. For each paragraph, circle the number of the topic sentence that you think gives the main idea. Discuss your choices with your classmates.

Paragraph 1

- Was born a twin—very important to childhood
- Large family
- Always had a friend, felt secure
- Separation from twin sister at school was difficult

Topic Sentences

1. Because I was born a twin, I had a very different childhood from most people.
2. Because I had a twin sister, I felt secure.
3. I didn't like school because I was in different classes from my twin sister.

Paragraph 2	**Topic Sentences**
• Teenage years difficult	1. I wasn't popular as a teenager.
• Liked to read, was shy, not popular	2. As a teenager, I taught swimming on weekends.
• Was a good swimmer	3. My teenage years were very difficult at first, but they ended happily.
• Taught swimming on weekends	
• This gave me self-confidence	

 **8** Write two possible topic sentences for your paragraph. Show the notes for your paragraph and your topic sentences to another student. Which one does he/she think is better? Why? Which one do you think is better? Why?

_____

_____

_____

Writing Titles

The title should give the main idea of a composition. It should also be interesting. It goes on the top line of the paper and is not a complete sentence.

In the title, capitalize the first word and all the important words. Don't capitalize the following kinds of words (unless they're the first word in the title):

■ conjunctions: *and, but, or, so*

■ articles: *the, a, an*

■ short prepositions: *at, by, for, in, of, on, out, to, up, with*

9 Write these titles with the correct capitalization.

1. an exciting life   An Exciting Life _____

2. all's well that ends well   _____

3. a gift of hope   _____

4. the best years of my life   _____

5. going away   _____

6. a happy ending   _____

7. life in a new city   _____

8. best friends   _____

9. a new beginning   _____

10. a wonderful experience   _____

10 Look at the possible titles for the paragraphs about the twin. Put a checkmark by the titles that you like. Why do you like them?

Paragraph 1	**Paragraph 2**
My Childhood	Growing Up
Born a Twin	Unhappy Teens
Difficult School Years	Teenage Years
My Childhood as a Twin	Teaching Swimming

11 Look at your paragraph notes from activity 6 on page 66 and write two possible titles for your paragraph. Show the notes for your paragraph and your titles to another student. Which one does he/she think is better? Why? Which one do you think is better? Why?

_____

_____

PART 2 # Write

Developing Cohesion and Style

Using the Past Tense

> Because you are writing about events in the past, most of your sentences will be in the past tense.

1 Complete the following paragraph with the correct past tense forms of the verbs in parentheses. For the spelling of verbs with *-ed,* see Appendix 1, page 184.

Because I ___was___ (be) born a twin, I _____ (have) a very different

childhood from most people. There _____ (be) always someone to play with

and I always _____ (have) a friend. My mother said we _____ (feed)

each other, _____ (play) together, and _____ (cry) when strangers

came near. We _____ (do) everything together. When my sister _____

(need) special shoes, I _____ (want) them too. But life as a twin _____

(not be) always great. My mother _____ (be) always tired because she

_____ (work) so hard. My father _____ (say) he _____ (hate) to
₁₃ ₁₄ ₁₅

come home because with my older brother there _____ (be) three screaming
₁₆

babies in the house. Even now I think that when I get something I want, someone

else will go without.

2 Look at your paragraph notes and write sentences with past tense verbs about your
life. Compare your verbs with those of other students. Can you use any of their
words? Also be careful to use past tense verbs only for completed events; don't write
"I studied English for three years" if you are still studying English.

Combining Sentences with Time Words and because

- When you write a paragraph that describes events, you can use time
  words to combine sentences. Some common time words are *before, after,
  when,* and *as soon as.*

  Examples
  Before I started school, I was very happy.
  After I left high school, I got a job.
  When my family said good-bye, I was very sad.
  As soon as I came to the United States, I got sick.

- You can also combine sentences with *because* to show reasons.

  Examples
  Because she worked hard, my mother was always tired.

- To review how to combine sentences with *and, but,* or *so,* see
  Chapter 1.

3 Complete the following paragraph with *before,
after, when, as soon as, because, and, but,* or *so.*

I had a typical childhood _____but_____ my
₁

life changed _____ I was fourteen. We
₂

moved from our small village to Karachi, a big

city in Pakistan. _____ we moved, life
₃

in the country was wonderful for me, but

_____ I started school in Karachi, I
₄

became shy and nervous. Some of the other

girls in my classes were mean _____ they laughed at my country ways.
5

_____ I didn't fit in, I became more interested in books. I always liked
6

biology, _____ I started to read about medicine. I was very unhappy at
7

the time, _____ I'm glad this happened _____ I finally
8   9

decided to become a doctor.

4   Finish these sentences. Use information about your life if you can.

1. When I became a teenager, I _started piano lessons_____.

2. I decided to study English because _____.

3. When I was a child, I _____.

4. After I left high school, I _____.

5. Before I started this class, _____.

6. I wasn't very happy, but _____.

Punctuating Sentences with Dependent Clauses

■   When you add a time word or *because* to a sentence, it becomes a
dependent clause. A dependent clause cannot stand alone—it is a
sentence fragment.

Examples

When I was five.
Because my father had a new job. } sentence fragments

■   You must combine a dependent clause with an independent clause—a
clause that can stand alone.

Example

We moved to Caracas.

■   If the dependent clause appears at the beginning of a sentence, use a
comma after it.

Examples

When I was five, we moved to Caracas.
Because my father had a new job, we moved to Caracas.

■   If the dependent clause appears at the end of the sentence, don't use a
comma in front of it.

Examples

We moved to Caracas when I was five.
We moved to Caracas because my father had a new job.

5   Combine the sentences with the word in parentheses. Use correct punctuation. It may be necessary to change the order of the sentences.

1.   I was a good student. I got a scholarship. (because)

     I got a scholarship because I was a good student.

2.   I graduated from high school. I was sixteen. (before)

     _____

3.   My father died. My mother went to work. (after)

     _____

4.   I found a job. I finished high school. (as soon as)

     _____

5.   I stopped studying. I was unhappy. (when)

     _____

6   Look at your paragraph notes and use each of the words below to write one sentence about your life. Be sure to use correct punctuation.

because   _____

before   _____

after   _____

when   _____

as soon as   _____

Writing the First Draft

7   Now write your paragraph about a part of your life. Use the topic sentence and the notes you wrote. Combine some sentences with time words and *because, and, but,* and *so.* Remember to use the past tense when you write about completed actions.

| PART 3 | # Edit and Revise |

Editing Practice

1 Some of these sentences have correct punctuation and some don't. Write *correct* after the sentence if the punctuation is correct. Rewrite the sentence with correct punctuation if it is wrong.

1. *Before* we moved here we used to have many friends and relatives nearby.

   _____

   _____

2. *Because* my uncle was an engineer, he sent me to engineering school.

   _____

   _____

3. I left the farm, *as soon as* I could

   _____

   _____

4. We moved to Colorado. *Because* the doctors said I needed a dry climate.

   _____

   _____

5. *When* I first came here, I loved the excitement of New York.

   _____

   _____

6. I came to the city, *when* I was five.

   _____

   _____

2   Edit this paragraph twice and rewrite it correctly. The first time, see where you can combine sentences with *and, but,* and *so.* (Remember to use correct punctuation.) The second time, correct past tense verb forms. Make any other changes you think are necessary.

---

how i became a jazz musician

I fall in love with jazz when I am five years old. I always heared jazz in the streets but for my fifth birthday my brother tooks me to a concert. There I saw a great saxophonist I decided to learn to play the saxophone. First I need a saxophone, I ask my father. My father say he no have money for a saxophone. I work for my brother, uncles, and cousins. I made a little money then my father see I work hard. He gave me money for a saxophone. I listen to recordings. My brother teach me. I practice every day. Soon I am a good saxophone player.

Editing Your Writing

3   Edit your paragraph using the following checklist.

Editing Checklist

1. Content
   a. Is the information interesting?
   b. Is the information important?
   c. Is there an interesting title?
2. Organization
   a. Does the topic sentence give the main idea of the paragraph?
   b. Are all the sentences about one topic?
   c. Should you change the order of any of the sentences?
3. Cohesion and Style
      Did you combine sentences with time words and *and, but, so,* and *because*?
4. Grammar
   a. Are your nouns, pronouns, and articles correct?
   b. Did you use complete sentences (no sentence fragments)?
   c. Did you use the correct past tense verbs?
5. Form
   a. Did you use correct paragraph form?
   b. Did you capitalize the words in the title correctly?
   c. Did you use correct punctuation when you combined sentences?

Peer Editing

4 Exchange paragraphs with another student. Discuss the paragraphs. Are there any other changes you should make?

Writing the Second Draft

5 Rewrite your paragraph using correct form. Then give it to your teacher for comments.

Using Feedback

Look at your teacher's comments. If you don't understand something, ask about it. Then look at all the paragraphs you wrote before and the teacher's comments on them. Make a list of goals for improving your writing. Use the following questions to help you write your goals.

1. Are your paragraphs interesting?
2. Are your ideas clear?
3. Are you organizing your paragraphs well?
4. Are you using good topic sentences?
5. Are there any grammatical structures you need to practice?
6. Do you need to use neater handwriting?
7. Is your spelling correct?
8. Are you using correct paragraph form?
9. How are your punctuation and capitalization?
10. Are you trying to write sentences that are too difficult?

What Do You Think?

Thinking about Birth Order

Many people believe that the birth order of children in a family affects the kind of people that they become. For example, people say that the eldest (firstborn) child is often more independent and a better leader.

What do you think? What is your birth order in your family? Has it affected you? How? Write for ten minutes in your journal. Then discuss what you wrote with your classmates.

| **PART 4** | # A Step Beyond |

Expansion Activities

1 If you want, let other students read your paragraph. You may want to show them pictures of you and your family, too. Discuss the experiences you wrote about. Did other students have similar experiences? Do you have questions about the other students' paragraphs?

2 Interview a friend or a relative about her or his life. Then choose one part and write about it.

3 Invent a life for yourself. Write about how you wish your life had been. Use the past tense.

Example   I was born into a very rich family. We lived in Venice for eight years. Then we moved to Florence.

Journal Writing

4 Write in your journal for ten minutes about one of the following topics.

1. The happiest time in my life
2. The saddest time in my life

Video Activities: Asthma and Dust Mites

Before You Watch.   Discuss these questions in a group.

1. What do you know about asthma? Tell what you know about the causes and the treatment of this condition.
2. Can you guess what a "dust mite" is?
3. How can people reduce the amount of dust in their houses?

Watch.

1. Write words to describe Linda Vine's house.

   _clean_____

2. How big do you think dust mites are? _____

3. In Linda Vine's house, you won't find

   a. dust   b. dust mites   c. anything made of cloth

4. Write four things Linda Vine does to control dust mites in her house.

   _____

5. What is an easy way to kill dust mites on bedding?

   _____

Watch Again.   Discuss these questions in a group.

1. The announcer says, "Asthma is part genetic and part environment." What does this mean? Can you think of other medical problems like this?
2. Did you know about dust mites before you saw this video?
3. If you had asthma, would it be difficult for you to change your house like Linda Vine did?

After You Watch.   The paragraph below was written by a student with asthma. Edit this paragraph twice. First, combine some sentences with *and, so,* and *because.* Then, correct errors in punctuation and past tense forms. Finally, re-write the paragraph.

---

how I discovered origami

Origami is the Japanese art of paper folding. I begin to learn it, when I am five years old. At that time I could not play outside, I had terrible asthma. One day I was very lonely. And my mother came home with a package of colored papers. She show me how to make a cute little dog just by folding the paper in a special way. Then she teach me how to make a frog and other animals. From that day I fell in love with origami. It become my friend When I was sick. Today my asthma is better. I can go to school. But, origami is still my hobby.

Chapter 6

Cultures of the World

PART 1

Before You Write

Exploring Ideas

Folktales

> Every culture has its own folktales. These stories tell us a lot about the culture in earlier times. Folktales are not written by one person. They also are not written at one time. Each story develops over many years. In this way, folktales come from the imagination of the whole culture.
>
> Folktales are usually told in time sequence. There is not usually a lot of description. Since the stories were told aloud, a simple story line helped the memory of both the storyteller and the listener.

1 Read the beginning of this folktale from Saxony, a part of Germany.

A powerful king was once lost in a forest. It was late at night. He was tired, cold, and hungry. He at last reached the hut of a poor miner. The miner was working and his wife was home alone. She was cooking potatoes on the fire when she heard someone at the door.

The king asked her for help. "We are very poor," she explained, "but we can give you potatoes for dinner and a blanket on the floor for a bed." The king gratefully accepted the kind old woman's offer. He sat down to dinner with her and ate a large plate of potatoes. "These are better than the best beef," he exclaimed. Then he stretched out on the floor and quickly fell asleep.

Early the next morning, the king washed in the river and then returned to the hut. He thanked the woman for her kindness and gave her a gold coin. Then he left.

As soon as the miner returned home, his wife told him about the visitor. Then she showed her husband the gold coin. The husband realized that the visitor was the king. However, he felt that the gold coin was too generous. He decided to take a bushel of potatoes to the king.

The miner went to the palace to see the king. "Your majesty," he said, "last night you gave my wife a gold coin for a hard bed and a plate of potatoes. You were too generous. Therefore, I have brought you a bushel of potatoes, which you said were better than the best beef. Please accept them."

The miner's words pleased the king. He wanted to reward him for his honesty, so he gave him a beautiful house and a small farm. The miner was very happy and he returned to tell his wife the news.

The poor miner had a brother. His brother was rich but greedy and jealous of anyone who had good luck. When he heard his brother's story, he was very upset.

Building Vocabulary

2   Find the words that mean:

1. small house   _hut_ _____

2. a large basket for vegetables   _____

3. selfish   _____

4. a person who digs for coal   _____

5. unselfish   _____

6. a kind of meat   _____

7. the home of a king   _____

8. envious   _____

3   Look at these pictures and choose the ending of the story. (If you want, you can make up your own ending.)

4   Make notes for an ending for the story, but do not write it yet. Use these questions as a guide.

1. What did the brother decide to give the king?
2. Was the king happy with the brother?
3. What did the king do?
4. How did the brother feel?

Organizing Ideas

Using a Time Sequence

> Writers use time words such as *before*, *after*, *as*, *when*, *while*, *then*, and *as soon as* to organize the information in a story.

5   Look at the story again. Make a list of the time words. Compare your list with another student's. Are there any words you missed?

_____   _____

_____   _____

_____   _____

_____   _____

_____   _____

_____   _____

_____   _____

Limiting Information

> Remember that it is important to limit what you say. If you include many unnecessary details, your reader or listener will lose interest in your story.

6   Look at your notes. Tell your story to another student, and discuss these questions.

1. Is my ending too complicated or difficult for the reader to understand?
2. Did I include too much description?
3. Can I fit everything into one paragraph?

Writing a Title

> The title of a story should be interesting and not too general, but it should not tell the reader how the story will end.

7   Which of the following do you think is a good title? Circle the number. Why do you think it's good?

1.   The Miner and the King
2.   Generous Brother and Selfish Brother
3.   A Gift for a Gift
4.   The Magic Potatoes

8   Give your story a title. You may use one of the above or make up your own.

PART 2   # Write

Developing Cohesion and Style

Using when *and* while *with the Past Continuous and the Simple Past Tenses*

> ■   If you want to talk about two actions in the past and one action interrupts the other, use *when* to introduce the interrupting action.
>
> **Example**
> The woman was cooking *when* the king knocked on the door.
>
> ■   Use *while* to introduce the action in progress, the action that was happening.
>
> **Example**
> *While* the woman was cooking, the king knocked on the door.
>
> ■   Use *while* to describe two actions in progress at the same time.
>
> **Example**
> *While* the miner was working, his wife was helping the king.
>
> ■   Use *when* if one action follows the other.
>
> **Example**
> *When* the miner's brother heard the story, he got jealous.

1   Combine these sentences with *when* or *while*. More than one answer may be correct.

1.   The king was hunting. He got lost in the forest.

_____

2.   The king saw the hut. He decided to ask for help.

_____

3.   The miner was talking to the king. His wife was working at home.

_____

4.   The miner gave the potatoes to the king. The king was pleased.

_____

5.   The king gave the woman the coin. She was surprised.

_____

2   Look at the notes for your story and write three sentences: two with *when* and one with *while*.

_____

_____

_____

Using as soon as

Use *as soon as* to emphasize that one action happened immediately after another.
Examples
> *As soon as* the miner got home, his wife told him the story.
> The miner ran home to tell his wife *as soon as* the miner received the gift from the king.

3   Combine these sentences with *as soon as*.

1.   The brother heard the story. He decided to give the king a better gift.

_____

2.   The king talked to the brother. He knew that he was a liar.

_____

3. The king ate dinner. He fell asleep.

_____

4. The miner got the farm. He quit his job.

_____

4 Look at the notes for your story and write two sentences with *as soon as.*

_____

_____

Using then

You can use *then* when you are narrating a story: By using *then,* you can make the time sequence clear and not repeat the same words. Compare:

Examples

I ran out of the house. After I ran out of the house, I saw a man in the street.

I ran out of the house. *Then* I saw a man in the street.

5 Rewrite these sentences using *then.*

1. The king washed in the river. He thanked the woman and left.

_____

2. The woman gave the king a plate of potatoes. She gave him a blanket.

_____

3. The king gave the woman a coin. He gave the miner a house and a farm.

_____

4. The brother found a bushel of potatoes. He took them to the king.

_____

Varying Time Words and Phrases

Now you have learned several different time words:

when   *while*   *as*   *before*   *after*   *then*   *as soon as*

Although these words do not have exactly the same meaning, you can use some of them in place of others.

Examples

When he got home, he heard the story.

He heard the story *as soon as* he got home.

After he got home, he heard the story.

He got home. *Then* he heard the story.

He got home *before* he heard the story.

To make your writing more interesting, it is important to vary the words you use.

6 Complete the sentences with the time words listed in the box.

1. _____When_____ the brother heard the story, he got jealous.

2. _____ the king met the second brother, he knew he was not sincere.

3. The miner and his wife were very happy _____ the king gave them the house.

4. The king left the miner's house, _____ the miner returned home.

5. _____ the second brother got the king's gift, he was very angry.

6. The king gave the old woman some gold. _____ he left.

Using Quotations

A good story tells the reader what the characters are thinking and saying.

- When you write exactly what someone said or thought, you use quotation marks. Use quotation marks in pairs. Use one set at the beginning of the quotation and one at the end.
- A quotation is always set off from the rest of the sentence by a comma, a question mark, or an exclamation point.
- The first word of a quote always starts with a capital letter.

Examples:

"It's not fair that he had such good luck," thought the miner's brother.

"We are very poor," the woman said, "but we can give you potatoes for dinner."

"I am lost and hungry. Can I have dinner and a place to sleep?" asked the king.

7 Look at these sentences. Put quotation marks and punctuation marks in the correct places. Change letters to capitals if you need to.

1. The king was too generous said the miner.
2. Why did you bring me this bushel of potatoes asked the king.
3. The king thought this man is very honest.
4. I'm sorry that we don't have any meat for you to eat said the woman.

8 Underline the sentences in the story that tell you what people are thinking and saying. Then look at the notes for your paragraph again. Write the conversation between the king and the brother.

Writing the First Draft

9 Now write your ending to the folktale. Remember to follow these three guidelines:

1. Use time words where they are necessary.
2. Limit the information. Your story should be one paragraph of 100 to 150 words.
3. Use quotations.

PART 3

Edit and Revise

Editing Practice

Using Editing Symbols

There are some common editing symbols that your teacher or your classmates may use. In Chapter 1 you learned about the caret (^). Here are some other symbols and examples of how they are used.

sp wrong spelling

>   sp
> He is a studint in Texas. → He is a student in Texas.

sf sentence fragment

>   sf
> When I was ten. We moved to New York. →
>
> When I was ten, we moved to New York.

/ use lowercase (small letters)

> The
> ^ Thief ran out the door. → The thief ran out the door.

⃪ take out this word, letter, or punctuation

> Sylvia sang a song,/while she washed the dishes. →
>
> Sylvia sang a song while she washed the dishes.

o add punctuation here

> The doctor arrived at ten o'clock₀ →
>
> The doctor arrived at ten o'clock.

1 Edit the following paragraph twice. The first time, check that all the information is really important. The paragraph has about 230 words. It should have about 150 to 170 words. Are there any sentences you can take out? The second time, check that the writer has used time expressions correctly. Make any other changes you think are necessary.

When he was riding home through the forest, he thought of a plan. "I'll give the king my best horse, he thought, then he will have to give me an even better gift!" As soon as breakfast the next day, he went to the palace. The palace was not far from his house. When he got to the palace. He asked to see the king. Tell him I have a present for him, he said. The guard immediately took him to see the king. Your majesty," he said, you know I have the best horses in the land. As king, you should have the best of my horses. If you look out the window, you will see my finest horse in your courtyard." The horse was magnificent. It was a big, black stallion. The king knew that this was not an honest gift. He smiled and said, "Thank you my friend. I accept your kind gift. Now I am going to give you a gift in return. Do you see that bushel of potatoes in the corner? Well those potatoes cost me a house and a farm. I am sure that they are the most expensive potatoes in the land. I would like you to have them." What could the greedy brother do? He lifted the heavy bushel and sadly left the room. As he was leaving, he heard the king laughing.

Editing Your Writing

2   Edit your paragraph using the following checklist.

Editing Checklist

1. Content
   a. Is the story clear?
   b. Is all the information important?

2. Organization
   a. Did you use time words where necessary?
   b. Did you add a title?

3. Cohesion and Style
   a. Did you vary the time words and expressions?
   b. Did you include enough description?
   c. Did you use quotations?

4. Grammar
   a. Did you use the correct forms of the past tense?
   b. Did you use the correct forms of the present continuous tense?
   c. Did you use good sentence structure (no fragments)?

5. Form
   a. Did you use commas correctly?
   b. Did you use quotation marks correctly?

Peer Editing

3   Exchange paragraphs with another student. Use editing symbols to edit each other's paragraphs. Discuss your paragraphs. Are there any other changes you should make?

What Do You Think?

Evaluating Folktales as Teaching Tools

Most folktales teach a lesson or moral. The real ending of this folktale is the paragraph on page 87. Reread the paragraph. What does this folktale tell us about German culture in the past? What is the moral of this story? Do you think it teaches it well? Are these kinds of stories still effective in passing down wisdom from generation to generation? What other things do our cultures today use to pass down ideas?

Writing the Second Draft

4   Write the second draft of your paragraph using correct form. Then give it to your teacher for comments.

PART 4

A Step Beyond

Expansion Activities

1   Read your ending to the other students in the class.

2   Write the beginning of a folktale that you know. Give it to a classmate. She or he will write the ending.

3   Rewrite a story that you know. It can be a famous story. It can be from a book or a movie. You can change the story if you wish.

4   Write a story based on your life. However, don't write it as your life. Write as if it happened to someone else.

Journal Writing

5   Write about the meaning of a folktale that you know.

Video Activities: Chinese New Year

Before You Watch.   Discuss these questions in a group.

1. Have you ever seen a Chinese New Year celebration? Describe this experience.
2. Talk about your New Year celebration last year. Where were you? Who was with you? How did you celebrate? Was it a happy time for you?

Watch.   Write answers to these questions.

1. In which season is the Chinese New Year? _____

2. Who is the blond woman? _____

3. Which Chinese customs did you see in the video? _____

_____

Watch Again.

1. How is the man going to celebrate the Chinese New Year? Place a check next to the things he says.
    _____ Eat
    _____ Drink alcohol
    _____ Buy gifts for his children
    _____ See dancing
    _____ Light firecrackers

2. Complete this sentence: "Some men are doing the Red Lion Dance. They dance for _____. If the _____ likes the dance, he gives them _____ envelopes with lucky _____ inside."

3. Why do people light firecrackers on the New Year?

4. The New Year celebrations will continue for _____ days.

After You Watch.   People in many cultures celebrate on the evening of December 31.

1. Think about last December 31. Where were you? Who was with you? Were you doing something special? Write a paragraph. Use the past and past continuous tenses. You may begin like this: "On December 31, 200_, I was _____."

2. Exchange papers with a partner. Check your partner's use of (a) verb tenses, and (b) punctuation.

3. Rewrite your paragraph and give it to your teacher. Be sure to give your paper a title.

Chapter 7

Health

IN THIS CHAPTER

You will write a paragraph about traditional health treatments.

PART 1

Before You Write

Exploring Ideas

Discussing Modern and Traditional Remedies

1 Look at the pictures below and discuss them. What kinds of treatments are shown? What do you think of these treatments?

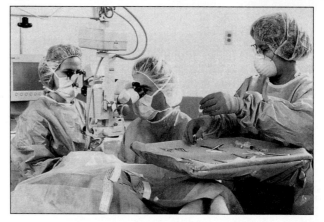

2 Discuss the following questions in small groups.

1. What do you do when you have a cold? Do you think modern treatments or traditional treatments are better?

2. What other traditional treatments do some people use? What do you think of them?

Building Vocabulary

3   The chart below has examples of vocabulary you can use to talk about health. What other new words can you add from your discussion? Look up the meanings of any new words.

Nouns	Verbs	Adjectives	Other
treatment	treat	effective	_____
acupuncture	heal	safe	_____
needles	take (medicine)	painful	_____
symptoms	massage	herbal	_____
healer	relieve	_____	_____
herbs	cure	_____	_____
pain	_____	_____	_____
_____	_____	_____	_____

4   When a suffix *(-er, -tion)* is added to the end of a word, it usually changes the word's part of speech. Look at these examples:

The verb *teach* + *er* = *teacher* (a noun)
The noun *friend* + *ly* = *friendly* (an adjective)

Look at the list of words in Activity 3. Find four pairs of words that are related. Complete the chart below.

treat	+	*ment*	=	*treatment*	
	+		=		
	+		=		
	+		=		

Organizing Ideas

Making an Idea Map

5   To get your ideas on paper, make an "idea map." Write the words *Traditional Treatments* in the middle of a piece of paper. Then write all your ideas about that topic around the paper. Use as many of the words from the list above as you can. Connect the words that go together. Look at the following example of an idea map of traditional treatments popular in the United States and Canada.

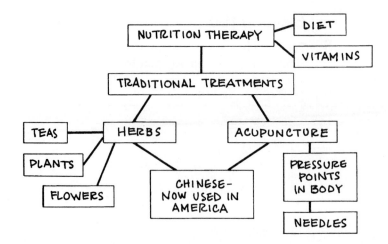

6 Look at your idea map and decide which type of paragraph you would like to write.

1. The different ways people use one kind of treatment

2. The different treatments people use for one illness

3. A short description of several different treatments you are familiar with

4. A thorough description of one type of treatment

7 Make a list of the ideas that you are going to use in your paragraph. Then evaluate your list. Use this checklist to help you.

	Yes	No	Maybe
1. The ideas are interesting.	❏	❏	❏
2. I have enough information for one paragraph.	❏	❏	❏
3. All the information will fit in one paragraph.	❏	❏	❏

Writing Topic Sentences

8 A: Circle the best topic sentence for a paragraph about herbs.

1. People often make teas with herbs to cure sore throats.

2. People use herbs to treat many different diseases.

3. I don't think herbs are as good as modern medicines.

B: Circle the best topic sentence for a paragraph about traditional treatments for colds.

1. You don't have to spend a lot of money at a pharmacy to treat a cold.

2. Lemon juice is a good traditional treatment for colds.

3. I had a horrible cold a year ago.

Now think of another topic sentence for this paragraph.

C: Circle the best topic sentence for a paragraph about several different traditional treatments popular in the United States and Canada.

1.   One traditional treatment people in the United States and Canada often use is massage.
2.   People in the United States and Canada often go to nutritionists.
3.   Many people in the United States and Canada are using traditional treatments instead of modern medicine to treat a variety of health problems.

Now think of another topic sentence for this paragraph.

9   Now write a topic sentence for your paragraph.

PART 2   # Write

Developing Cohesion and Style

Using Restrictive Relative Clauses

> Good writers combine short sentences with relative pronouns to make longer, more natural sentences. The relative pronoun *who* is used for people. The relative pronoun *that* is used for things and people.
>
> **Examples**
>
> There are many people in the United States and Canada.
>
> They are trying acupuncture. →
>
>   There are many people in the United States and Canada *who/that* are trying acupuncture.
>
> Aspirin is a very common medicine.
>
> Aspirin is used to treat headaches and colds. →
>
>   Aspirin is a very common medicine *that* is used to treat headaches and colds.
>
> Notice that *who* and *that* replace the subjects of the second sentences.

Chinese
acupuncture chart

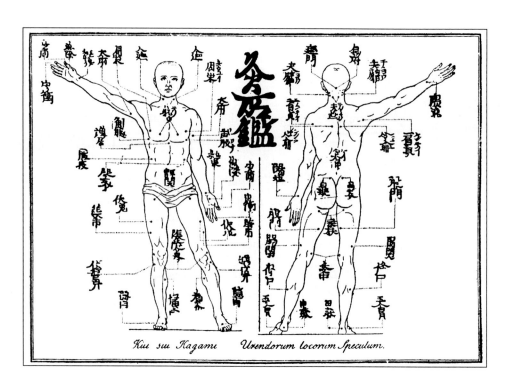

Kiu su Kagami   Urendorum locorum Speculum.

1 Combine these sentences with the relative pronoun *who* or *that*.

1. Acupuncture is an ancient treatment. This treatment developed in China.

   Acupuncture is an ancient treatment that developed in China.
   _____

2. An acupuncturist is a person. This person uses needles to treat diseases.

   _____

3. Many people find acupuncture helpful. They experience pain.

   _____

4. Acupuncturists also use herbs. These herbs help treat the problem.

   _____

2 Complete these sentences with relative clauses that begin with *who* or *that*.

1. There are many traditional remedies that can help you. _____

2. People _____ often use herbs to treat diseases.

3. I knew a woman _____

4. There are many plants _____

5. My friend goes to a doctor _____

6. My grandmother uses an herb _____

7. I know someone _____

8. There are some new medicines _____

9. I once used a traditional treatment _____

10. I once read a story about a man _____

Using Transitional Words and Phrases: in addition, for example, *and* however

Transitional words and phrases help unify a paragraph. They can be used to add information, give examples, or give contrasting information. They often come at the beginning of a sentence and are followed by a comma.

■ **Adding Information: in addition**

In addition is similar to *and* and *also*. Use *in addition* when you are adding information after a long sentence or after several sentences.

Example

People used to drink special teas to cure many illnesses. Herbalists made some of these teas from the bark of certain trees. *In addition*, they sometimes made a cream with certain kinds of bark to put on cuts and bruises.

■ **Giving Examples: for example**

Use *for example* when you want to give specific examples.

Example

Many people go to psychic healers. *For example*, my cousin went to a healer who cured his high fever with the touch of her hands.

■ **Giving Contrasting Information: however**

However is similar to *but*, but it often appears in more formal writing. It is used to give contrasting information.

Example

Some psychic healers can cure many diseases. *However*, others just take people's money and don't help them.

3 Complete the sentences with *in addition*, *for example*, or *however*.

1. There are many Chinese acupuncturists in Canada. Many of them studied acupuncture in China and then immigrated to Canada. _____, many Canadian doctors are now giving acupuncture treatments.

2. I often drink herbal teas when I am sick. _____, if I am very sick, I take modern medicine.

3. Some people in California use many traditional treatments from various parts of the world. _____, they use remedies and treatments from China.

4. My grandmother often goes to an old lady who gives her strange treatments. _____, these treatments don't usually help her.

5. I take lemon juice for colds. I put it in a cup of warm water and drink it several times a day. _____, I take it for sore throats and fevers.

4 After each sentence write another sentence that begins with *for example*, *in addition*, or *however*. Put commas after the transitional words.

1. I don't use traditional treatments.

    However, my sister thinks they are effective.

    _____

2. Many herbal teas are good for digestion.

    _____

    _____

3. She went to a nutritionist.

    _____

    _____

4. Psychologists can help you with many problems.

_____

_____

5. It's important to have healthful foods.

_____

_____

Showing Purpose and Giving Reasons

In Chapter 5, you learned how to use *because* to give reasons.

Example

> My mother went to an acupuncturist *because* she didn't like to take medicine.

An infinitive (*to* + verb) can also show reason or purpose.

Examples

> I drank herbal tea *to* cure my sore throat.
> He gave me a massage *to* help my back.
> The Chinese use acupuncture *to* stop pain.

5 Read this paragraph and answer the questions that follow.

You don't have to spend a lot of money at a pharmacy to treat a cold because there are many inexpensive old remedies that are just as good as the newer ones. For example, my grandmother always advised us to drink honey and lemon juice in hot water to cure coughs. People who study natural medicine now say that lemon juice is good for colds because it kills germs, and honey contains natural elements that improve health. In addition, my mother used a natural remedy to help me breathe better when I had a cold. She put me in a room full of steam. Doctors still recommend this remedy. Because scientists haven't found any easily available medicine that kills viruses which cause colds, there isn't any cure for the common cold. I therefore think honey, lemon juice, and steam are safer than chemicals with long names I can't pronounce.

1. Underline the reason why lemon juice is good for colds. What word introduces the reason?

   _____

2. Find a reason that comes at the beginning of a sentence. Circle it.

3. Find two examples of infinitive expressions that show purpose. Draw two lines under them.

Writing the First Draft

6 Now write your paragraph about traditional treatments. Give reasons and examples and show purpose when you can. Use these expressions:

1. Examples: *for example*
2. Reasons and purposes: *because*, *to* + verb
3. Additional reasons or examples: *in addition, also*

Give your opinion in the last sentence of your paragraph.

PART 3 # Edit and Revise

Editing Practice

Using Editing Symbols

> You learned some editing symbols in Chapter 6, page 86. Here are some more symbols your teacher may use.
>
> sp   The spelling is wrong.
>
> wt   The tense is wrong.
>
> ro   You wrote a *run-on* sentence. A run-on sentence is an incorrect sentence that should be two sentences.
>
> > ro
> > He ate only junk food and never exercises, in addition he stayed up late every night.
>
> ↻   You should move the circled part to where the arrow points.
>
> ≡   Capitalize the letter.
>
> ww   The word is wrong. Some words are almost synonyms, but each has special uses.
>
> > ww
> > I like to swim to rest.

1   Rewrite these sentences correctly.

1.   many people in the Philippines drink herb teas.

_____

2.   The healer gave (to my friend) a foot massage.

_____

   wt
3.   Three years ago he have a stomach ache.

_____

   ww
4.   His leg did not cure.

_____

   ro
5.   My friend didn't like to go to doctors, he went to a psychic.

_____

2   Edit this paragraph twice and rewrite it correctly. The first time, add transitional words and phrases such as *for example*, *however*, and *in addition*. The second time, add commas after transitional words and dependent clauses that begin sentences. Also use commas before conjunctions when you combine two complete sentences.

Some people can cure themselves of cancer with traditional treatments. I know a woman who cured herself of cancer by fasting. She didn't eat for one month and then she slowly began to eat again. When she completed the fast she had completely cured herself of cancer. I read about a man who cured his cancer using an old Chinese diet. As soon as he started the diet he began to get better. Scientists don't have a modern drug to cure cancer.

Editing Your Writing

3   Edit your paragraph using the following checklist.

Editing Checklist

1. Content
   a. Is the information interesting?
   b. Are there purposes and examples in the paragraph?
2. Organization
   a. Does the topic sentence give the main idea of the paragraph?
   b. Are all the sentences about the topic of the paragraph?
3. Cohesion and Style
   a. Did you use relative clauses correctly?
   b. Did you use transitional words and phrases correctly?
4. Grammar
   a. Did you use correct noun forms?
   b. Did you use correct verb forms?
5. Form
   Are there commas after transitional words and after dependent clauses?

Peer Editing

4   Exchange papers with another student and edit each other's writing. You can use some of the editing symbols you learned in Chapter 6, page 86 and on page 100 of this chapter.

Herbal shop

Focus on Testing

Recognizing Correct Usage of Transitional Phrases

This is a new section that helps you with skills for taking writing tests, including standardized tests such as the TOEFL. Recognizing the correct usage of transitional phrases is often tested in a multiple-choice format. The following activity will give you practice using this format.

5   Choose the answer below that best completes the sentence.

Jethro Kloss was an herbalist who treated many Americans who doctors couldn't help. _____ he wrote an important book about traditional treatments. Mr. Kloss encouraged the use of natural remedies. _____ he said that a good diet with plenty of fruit and vegetables was very important. He _____ advised his patients to get a lot of activity. Because he knew about hundreds of herbs, he was one of the most famous herbalists in the United States.

1.	2.	3.
(a) In addition,	(a) For example	(a) however
(b) For example,	(b) Example,	(b) in addition
(c) However,	(c) For example,	(c) too
(d) Because	(d) example	(d) also

Writing the Second Draft

6   Rewrite your paragraph using correct form. Then give it to your teacher for comments. When your teacher returns your paragraph, look at his or her comments. Do you understand your teacher's editing symbols? If there are symbols you don't understand, ask your teacher about them.

PART 4   A Step Beyond

Expansion Activities

1   Your class can make a short book of traditional treatments throughout the world. Type or write your paragraphs neatly and put them together in a folder or binder. Some students can draw or find pictures for the book. You can pass the book around the class or give it to another English class to read.

2   Write about an illness or health problem you or a family member has or had. Describe the illness. How are/were you treating the problem? Are/were you getting good health care?

Journal Writing

3   Write in your journal for ten minutes about one or more of the following topics.

1.   Things to do to stay healthy
2.   How I keep my good health/What I do that is bad for my health
3.   The oldest person I know

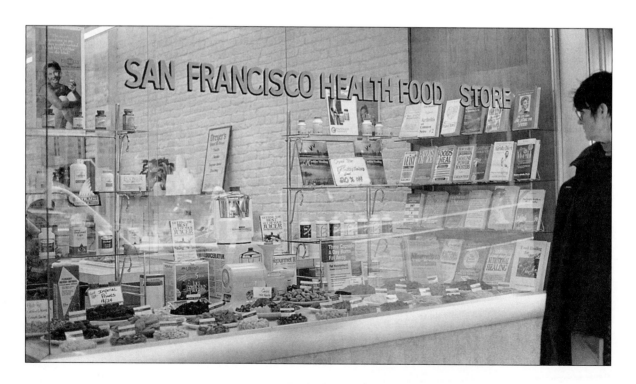

What Do You Think?

1. In what ways are modern and traditional medicine different? What features can you find in both? List them in the following chart. Use the features listed here and others you can think of. Remember that different people may have different opinions about whether something is a feature of modern or traditional medicine. Give reasons for your choices.

   - Is expensive/is inexpensive
   - Requires formal training to practice/doesn't require formal training to practice
   - Is dangerous/is not dangerous
   - Can be used to treat serious diseases/can't be used to treat serious diseases
   - Is natural/is artificial
   - Is controlled by the government/isn't controlled by the government
   - Can be used to cheat people/can't be used to cheat people

   Traditional medicine   **Modern medicine**

   _____   _____

   _____   _____

   _____   _____

   _____   _____

   _____   _____

   _____   _____

   _____   _____

2. Write in your journal or discuss which you think is better—traditional or modern medicine. Use the features in the chart to give reasons for your opinion.

Video Activities: Marathon Man

Before You Watch.   Discuss these questions in a group.

1. What is a marathon?
2. Do you think you could run in a marathon?
3. Why do some people run or jog? Make a list of reasons.
4. Do you enjoy running? Why or why not?

Watch.   Write answers to these questions.

1. What is Jerry's personal reason for running? _____

    _____

2. Does he enjoy it? _____

3. What does Jerry want to challenge Americans to do? _____

    _____

Watch Again.   Fill in the missing numbers.

1. How many miles is a marathon?   _____
2. How many marathons did Jerry run in 1993?   _____
3. How many marathons does Jerry hope to run in 2000?   _____
4. How many marathons has he run so far?   _____
5. How fast does Jerry run a marathon?   _____

After You Watch.   It takes Jerry 4 hours and 45 minutes to run a marathon, and he plans to run 200 marathons this year. This means that Jerry runs about 2.6 hours a day, or about 18 hours a week.

Write a paragraph answering this question: If you could choose an enjoyable and healthy activity to do 18 hours a week, what would it be? Why?

Chapter 8

Entertainment and the Media

You will write a paragraph about your favorite movie.

PART 1	# Before You Write

Exploring Ideas

Describing and Categorizing Movies

1 Look at the photos from these movies and match them with the movie categories below.

musical	comedy	horror
science fiction	drama	action

1.

Mission Impossible

Category: _action_

2.

Chicken Run

Category: _____

3.

Star Wars

Category: _____

4.

Evita

Category: _____

5.

6.

Life Is Beautiful

Scream

Category: _____

Category: _____

2 Discuss these questions in small groups.

1. What kind of movie do you like best?

2. What kind of movie do you like least?

3. What is your favorite movie? Who are the stars of that movie? Who are the main characters? What type of movie is it? When and where does it take place?

Building Vocabulary

3 Circle the adjectives that describe your favorite movie.

exciting	realistic	action-packed
funny	sad	well-written
fascinating	imaginative	well-directed
horrifying	touching	frightening
interesting	entertaining	heartwarming

4 Look at the list of adjectives that describe people. Put a checkmark (✔) next to the positive characteristics and an X next to the negative characteristics. Put a question mark if you are not sure. Use your dictionary to help you.

crazy	talkative	loyal
funny	brawny	smart
angry	shy	brilliant
evil	talented	stocky
fun-loving	ambitious	hardworking
brave	kind	successful
childlike	sexy	gorgeous
courageous	handsome	well-built
innocent	stubborn	independent
egotistical	ordinary	

5   Who is your favorite character in the movie? What is he or she like? Circle the
adjectives that describe him or her.

6   List any other adjectives that describe this character.

_____	_____	_____
_____	_____	_____
_____	_____	_____
_____	_____	_____

Organizing Ideas

Summarizing a Movie Plot

> When you write about your favorite movie, you will include a summary of the
> plot. A good way to do this is to first write a list of events from the movie and
> then to choose the most important and interesting events to include in your
> summary.

7   Look at the following list of events from the movie *Titanic*. Then write a similar
list of events in your favorite movie. Don't worry about grammar or form. If
there are any words you don't know in English, write them in your native
language. You can look them up in a dictionary later if you choose to include the
event in your summary.

1. Jack wins a ticket on the Titanic in a card game.
2. Jack sees Rose on the ship.
3. Rose tries to commit suicide and Jack saves her.
4. Rose invites Jack to dinner.
5. Rose's fiancé, Cal Hockley, gives her a diamond necklace.
6. Rose and Jack go dancing with his friends.
7. Cal's friend tells him that Rose and Jack were together.
8. Cal gets angry with Rose.
9. Jack steals a coat and goes to find Rose.
10. Jack draws Rose's picture. They put the picture in the safe.
11. Jack and Rose see the iceberg that hits the ship.
12. Cal's friends put the diamond necklace in Jack's pocket. Then they accuse
    him of being a thief.

13. Jack is arrested and locked in a room.
14. The ship begins to sink.
15. Rose helps Jack escape.
16. Jack and Cal put Rose onto a lifeboat.
17. Rose jumps back onto the ship to be with Jack.
18. Rose and Jack jump into the water.
19. They find something to float on but it won't hold both of them.
20. Jack dies in the water. Rose is saved.

Including Important Information in a Summary

A good movie summary should be more than a list of events. It also tells the problem and events leading to a solution. In addition, a good movie summary includes only important events—the ones that relate the problem and the solution. Finally, a good movie summary shows the relationship between important events.

You can show the relationship between two events by using words such as *when, while, so, but, and, because,* and so on.

Examples

While Rose and Jack are together, an iceberg hits the ship.

Rose is very grateful, *so* she invites Jack to dinner.

Cal accuses Jack of stealing the necklace *and* he is arrested.

Rose gets into a lifeboat *but* she can't leave Jack.

8 Read the following two summaries of *Titanic*. Which is the better summary of the movie? Why? Think about these questions:

■ What is the problem in the movie *Titanic*? What is the solution?

■ Which paragraph includes the important events that show the problem and the solution?

■ Which paragraph explains the story more clearly?

The movie *Titanic* is a love story which takes place in the middle of a disaster. Rose DeWitt Bukater is a beautiful young woman. She is returning to the United States with Caledon Hockley and her mother. Rose is engaged to Hockley. Her mother wants her to marry him because he is rich. Rose is very unhappy because she doesn't love Hockely. One night, she gets upset and tries to commit suicide. Jack Dawson, a poor young artist saves her life. Rose is very grateful, so she invites Jack to a formal dinner. After dinner, he takes her dancing in the part of the ship where all the poor people are. Rose has a wonderful time. She and Jack fall in love. The next day they meet in secret. While they are together, an iceberg hits the ship. Meanwhile, a friend of Cal's puts a diamond necklace in Jack's pocket. Cal accuses Jack of stealing the necklace and he is arrested. The ship begins to sink. Rose fights her way down to Jack and helps him to escape. There are not enough lifeboats. Rose gets onto a lifeboat but she can't leave Jack. She jumps back onto the ship. Right before the ship sinks, Rose and Jack jump into the water. They find a piece of wood that is floating but it is not large enough for both of them. Jack stays in the water. He dies from the cold. Rose is saved.

The movie, *Titanic* is basically a love story. The main characters are Rose, a beautiful upper-class young woman and Jack, a poor young artist. Rose is on the Titanic with her mother and her fiancé, Cal. By chance, Rose and Jack meet and fall in love. Then the ship begins to sink. Rose saves Jack's life. Then they jump off the ship together. Unfortunately, Jack dies but Rose survives.

9 Look at the list of events you wrote from your favorite movie. Work in groups or pairs. Which events are the most important? Are there any events that you can combine to show their relationship?

10 The paragraph that follows includes all the information in the list below. Read the paragraph, find all the information listed, and write it on the lines.

1. The type of movie   _____
2. Where the movie takes place _____
3. When the movie takes place   _____
4. The problem   _____
5. The result   _____
6. The main characters   _____
7. Why you like the movie   _____

E. T.: The Extra-Terrestrial: A Heartwarming Adventure

One of my favorite movies is *E. T.: The Extra-Terrestrial*, a touching science fiction story about the friendship of a young boy and E. T., a creature from outer space. It takes place in the 1980s in a small American town. When E. T.'s spaceship leaves without him, he meets Elliot, a boy who becomes his friend. E. T. likes Elliot, but he is very homesick, so Elliot decides to help him contact his friends. This is not easy because some scientists are searching for E. T. in order to study him. Elliot and E. T. escape from the scientists by bicycle. They go to the woods to meet the spaceship that will take E. T. home, and in a beautiful scene, they say good-bye. I found everything I like best in movies in *E. T.* The characters are wonderful, and it has great suspense, a magical story, and an ending that moved me to tears.

11   Look at your list of events from your favorite movie. Make a list of any other information you would like to add.

Writing a Title

> If you give your paragraph an interesting title, people will want to read it. Titles of movies are underlined (or put in italics in printed material). All the important words in a title (of a movie, book, etc.) begin with a capital letter. Small words such as *and, in, a, the, to, at,* or *with* do not begin with a capital letter unless they are the first words in the title.
>
> **Examples**
>   The Story of Qui Ju
>   Dona Flor and Her Two Husbands

12   Punctuate the titles in parentheses and capitalize words that need capital letters.

1. You should see (the seven dwarfs), a classic Disney film.
   You should see The Seven Dwarfs, a classic Disney film.

2. The Spanish actor Chow Yung Fat was in (anna and the king).

3. The Italian movie (life is beautiful) won several awards.

4. Sandra Bullock starred in (while you were sleeping).

5. One of the most famous horror movies of all time is (the exorcist).

13   Look at the following titles. Which movies would you like to read about? Why?
1. *Incredible Voyage:* My Favorite Movie
2. *The Chinese Lantern:* An Unforgettable Experience
3. *Sam and Me:* A Good Movie

14   Write a title for your paragraph.

| PART 2 | # Write |

Developing Cohesion and Style

Using Adjectives

> One way to make a movie summary interesting is to add adjectives that describe characters and events.

1 Look back at the list of adjectives that describe movies in the Building Vocabulary section on page 109. The carets mark places to add adjectives. Think of appropriate adjectives and use them to rewrite the sentences.

1. *Star Wars* is a ˄ science-fiction movie.

   Star Wars is a realistic science-fiction movie.

2. *Dracula* is a ˄ horror movie about a ˄ vampire.

   _____

3. *Titanic* is a ˄ love story about a couple on a sinking ship.

   _____

4. *Schindler's List* is a ˄ drama about a German who saved the lives of many Jews.

   _____

2 Write a similar sentence about your favorite movie.

   _____

   _____

3 Make a list on the board of some of your favorite movie characters. Look back at the list of adjectives that describe movies in the Building Vocabulary section on page 109. In small groups, write phrases describing those characters using the adjectives on the list or other adjectives.

Examples

   E. T.—a magical visitor from another planet

   Rambo—a brawny ex-soldier

Using Appositives

You can combine sentences using appositives. In Chapter 3, you used appositives to describe foods. This structure is also useful here.

Examples

Han Solo is one of the heroes of *Star Wars*. He is a brave but egotistical pilot. →

Han Solo, a brave but egotistical pilot, is one of the heroes of *Star Wars*.

E. T. and *Jurassic Park* were directed by Steven Spielberg. He is one of America's most popular filmmakers. →

E. T. and *Jurassic Park* were directed by Steven Spielberg, one of America's most popular filmmakers.

4 Can you find any appositives in the paragraph about *E. T.: The Extra-Terrestrial*? Underline them.

5 Combine the following sentences by using appositives. Remember to use commas.

1. *Gone with the Wind* takes place in the south of the United States. It is a film about the U.S. Civil War.

   Gone with the Wind, a film about the U.S. Civil War, takes place in the south

   of the United States.

2. In *Jurassic Park*, the dinosaurs seem totally real. It is a comic and hair-raising thriller.

   _____

   _____

3. Cal Hockley is Rose's fiancé in *Titanic*. He is a rich but evil man.

   _____

   _____

4. *Life Is Beautiful* is about Jews in Italy during the Second World War. It is a funny and tragic movie.

   _____

   _____

5. In *Shakespeare in Love*, Gwyneth Paltrow plays a woman who pretends to be a man. She is a famous American actress.

   _____

   _____

Using the Historical Present Tense

> Look back at the paragraph about *E. T.: The Extra-Terrestrial.* What tense is it in? You can use the present tense to talk about movies that describe events in the past. This is the "historical present."

6 Look at the following paragraph and complete it with the correct forms of the verbs in parentheses. Use the historical present.

It's a Wonderful Life _____ (be) a heartwarming drama. In this movie,
1

James Stewart _____ (play) an ordinary family man who _____ (live)
2   3

in a small American town. When he is about to lose his business because of a

serious mistake, Stewart _____ (become) very depressed. He _____
4   5

(try) to jump off a bridge, but an angel _____ (show) him how important he
6

_____ (be) to his friends, family, and the community. He then _____
7   8

(decide) not to kill himself.

What Do You Think?

Choosing Movies

How do you choose the movies you see? What do your movie choices say about you as a person? To find out, try the following activity.

1. Here are some possible reasons for choosing a movie. Put a check (✔) next to the reasons that are important to you in choosing a movie. If you have other reasons, write them in the blanks.

   _____ the director

   _____ the actors

   _____ the story

   _____ music

   _____ the setting (where and when story takes place)

   _____ special effects

   _____ other: _____

   _____

2. Think about the last five movies you chose to see. They can be movies you saw in a theater, rented on video, or watched on TV. Write the names of these movies in the chart below. (Don't list movies you saw because someone else chose them!) Next to each movie, write your three most important reasons for choosing it. One movie is done for you as an example.

	Reasons for Choosing It		
Name of Movie	**Most Important**	**Very Important**	**Important**
1. Titanic	story	actors	special effects
2.			
3.			
4.			
5.			

3. When you finish, look at your list of movies and reasons. Do you see any similarities or patterns in your choices? For example, do you have a favorite actor or director? Do you like movies about different times in history? Do you usually choose movies for the same reason(s)?

4. Work with a partner. Exchange charts and look at your choices of movies. How are your choices and reasons similar or different? Did you see any of your partner's movies? Why or why not?

5. Write in your journal for five minutes about what you learned from this activity. Do you plan to see different kinds of movies in the future?

Writing the First Draft

7   Write the paragraph about your favorite movie. Use important events and information, and combine sentences to show the relationship between events. Also include adjectives and appositives to describe the movie and characters. Use the title you wrote. You can write the paragraph in the historical present tense.

PART 3	# Edit and Revise

Editing Practice

Using Two or More Adjectives

> ■ Sometimes you may want to use more than one adjective. You can separate two or more adjectives with a comma.
>
> **Examples**
> E. T. is a friendly, lovable creature from outer space.
> In the movie *Rocky,* the main character is a handsome, determined boxer.
>
> ■ When there are two contrasting adjectives, you can separate them with *but.*
>
> **Example**
> In *Star Wars,* Han Solo is a brave but egotistical pilot.

1 Look at these sentences. Put a comma between the two adjectives.

  1. *Gandhi* is the story of a wise kind man who leads India to freedom.

  2. In *It's a Wonderful Life,* James Stewart plays a hard-working ordinary man.

  3. *The 400 Blows* tells the story of a lonely unhappy boy.

  4. *Women on the Verge of a Nervous Breakdown* contains many colorful comic characters.

2 Put the word *but* in the appropriate places in the sentences.

  1. *Gandhi* is about a gentle powerful leader.

  2. *Frankenstein* is the story of a destructive tragic monster.

  3. *The Godfather* is about an evil loyal man.

  4. The lead characters in *Thelma and Louise* are vulnerable brave.

3 Edit the following paragraph twice and rewrite it correctly. The first time you edit, take out any unnecessary details. The second time, change the verbs to the historical present, correct punctuation, and make any other changes you think are necessary.

Star Trek II: **The Wrath of Khan**

Star Trek II is a science fiction film. *Star Trek* was first a television series, and this is the second *Star Trek* movie. In this movie, Khan, an evil but clever leader stole information about a secret government experiment. Leonard Nimoy played Mr. Spock. The crew of the spaceship *Enterprise* had to catch Khan before he could use the information. Captain Kirk and his crew succeeded as usual, but in the end, the captain lost a good friend. Which one of the crew died? See the movie and find out it's definitely a good film to watch. I liked this movie a lot. Maybe you will too.

Editing Your Writing

4   Edit your paragraph using the following checklist.

Editing Checklist

1. Content
   a. Is the title interesting?
   b. Would others want to see the movie because of your summary?
   c. Did you present the problem and the events leading to the solution?
   d. Does your summary include the type of movie, when and where the movie takes place, and the main characters?
2. Organization
   a. Is all the information in the paragraph important?
   b. Does the topic sentence give a general idea of what kind of movie you're writing about?
3. Cohesion and Style
   a. Did you combine sentences to show the relationship between events?
   b. Did you use appositives correctly?
   c. Did you use adjectives to describe the characters and the movie?
   d. Did you use the historical present tense?
4. Grammar
   a. Are the present tense verbs correct?
   b. Are the count and noncount nouns correct?
   c. Did you combine sentences correctly?
5. Form
   a. Did you underline the title of the movie?
   b. Did you use commas with appositives and adjectives correctly?
   c. Did you punctuate combined sentences correctly?

Peer Editing

5 Exchange papers with another student and edit each other's paragraphs.

Writing the Second Draft

6 After you and another student edit your paragraph, rewrite it using correct form. Then give it to your teacher for comments.

Focus on Testing

Summarizing

Summarizing can be a useful test-taking skill. You have been practicing this skill throughout the chapter, and making a summary of a movie is no different than making a summary of a book or other series of events. You must choose the important events, give the background, and relate the problem and the events leading to a solution. The following activity will give you more practice in writing summaries.

Timed Activity: 15 Minutes
With a partner, choose a book, movie, TV program, or historical or current event that you are both familiar with. Do not discuss it. Write your own summary. Then exchange summaries and compare them. How are they the same or different? Did your partner include information that you did not?

| PART 4 | # A Step Beyond |

Expansion Activities

1 Read three of your classmates' movie summaries. Discuss which movies you would like to see and why. If you have seen any of the movies, tell whether you agree with your classmates' summaries.

Journal Writing

2 Write in your journal for ten minutes about one or more of the following topics:

1. Violence in movies
2. Why I like (or don't like) movies
3. My favorite book
4. A current event

Video Activities: Quiz Shows

Before You Watch.

1. Circle the kinds of TV show you like to watch.

    a. comedies   b. dramas   c. quiz shows   d. soap operas

2. Do you like watching quiz shows on TV? Discuss with a partner.

3. Describe your favorite TV quiz show to your partner.

Watch.   Discuss the following questions with your classmates.

1. On all the game shows you saw in the videos, what must contestants do in order to win money?

2. Why do television networks like to make game shows?

3. The contestants on today's game shows are

    a. millionaires   b. ordinary people   c. scholars

Watch Again.   Write T if the statements below are true and F if they are false. Then correct all the false statements.

1. _____   In the U.S., you can watch a game show on TV almost every night of the week.

2. _____   Quiz shows are a new idea.

3. _____   The first game show in America was called "Who Wants to Be a Millionaire?"

4. _____   If a television show is successful, other networks hurry to copy it.

5. _____   Game shows are cheaper to make than sitcoms.

6. _____   In the short term, American TV networks will stop making game shows.

7. _____   The questions on the new "Twenty One" show are called "relatable." This means they are about families.

After You Watch.   Write instructions for playing a simple game. Use the present tense and words that show a time sequence (*before, after, first, next,* etc.) You may follow the model below. Edit your paper and rewrite it. Then read it to your classmates and have fun playing the game!

Example

How to Play Twenty Questions

I want to explain how to play a simple game called Twenty Questions. To begin, one person thinks of a famous person. The other players must guess who this person is. They are allowed to ask twenty questions about the famous person, but they must be yes/no questions. For example: "Is this person a man?" "Is he (she) American?" "Is he (she) younger than 30?" "Does he (she) play a musical instrument?" "Is he (she) a politician?" The game is over when the players guess correctly or when 20 questions are finished.

Chapter 9

Social Life

You will write about a classmate's life in the past year.

PART 1

Before You Write

Exploring Ideas

Interviewing Someone

1   In this chapter you are going to interview a classmate about his or her life in the past year. In groups, think of different topics to ask about. Add to the following list.

- ■ Family life
- ■ Social life
- ■ _____
- ■ _____
- ■ _____
- ■ _____

2   Write questions about the topics in Activity 1. Think of other questions you could ask a student in your class. Your teacher will list them on the board.

3   You have prepared to interview a classmate. Now prepare for someone to interview you by making a list of the things you have done in the past year. Think about the questions in Activity 2.

4   Use the questions from Activity 3 to interview a student about his or her life in the past year. Take notes on the information your partner gives you. When your partner interviews you, try to give him/her as much information as you can.

Building Vocabulary

5   The chart below has examples of vocabulary you can use to talk about life events. What other new words can you add from your discussions and interview? In small groups, discuss the meaning of any words you do not understand.

Nouns	Verbs	Adjectives	Other
career	accomplish	exhausted	be interested in
hobby	attend	fascinating	be used to
recreation	enjoy	surprising	_____
_____	_____	responsible	_____
_____	_____	difficult	_____
_____	_____	_____	_____
_____	_____	_____	_____
_____	_____	_____	_____

6 Complete the following chart by combining each verb and adjective in the first column with a suffix to form a noun. If necessary, use a dictionary to help you.

enjoy (verb)	+	*ment*	=	*enjoyment*
accomplish (verb)	+		=	
responsible (adjective)	+		=	
difficult (adjective)	+		=	

Organizing Ideas

You are going to write a paragraph about a student in your class for a class newsletter. The paragraph will say what the student has been doing for the past year.

Writing Topic Sentences

Topic sentences about what someone has been doing for the past year are often in the present perfect tense (*have/has* + past participle) or the present perfect continuous tense (*have/has* + *been* + verb + *ing*).

Examples

June Nomura *has lived* in Texas since April.

Ben Rodriguez *has been working* in a hospital.

7 Which of these sentences are good general topic sentences for a paragraph about someone's life during the past year? Circle the numbers of those sentences. Which sentence do you think is the most interesting? Put a check by it.

1. Tony Prado has been busy this year.

2. Reiko Suzuki has been married since June.

3. This year Paco Vega has had so much to do he has felt like a juggler.

4. Hilda Bronheim has learned a lot of English this year.

5. During the past year Li Yun Wen has gotten married, worked at two jobs, played soccer, and studied English.

6. During the past year Ana Leone has had a full but happy life.

A Juggler

 **8** Write a topic sentence for your paragraph. Use the present perfect or the present perfect continuous tense. Then show the sentence to the person that you interviewed. Does he/she agree with your topic sentence?

Organizing Information in a Paragraph

There are two ways to organize your paragraph:

1. You can begin with more important activities such as work, and you can end with less important activities such as hobbies or interesting events.
2. You can begin with difficult activities and end with more enjoyable activities.

 9 Look at the following notes about one student's life. Work in small groups and arrange them in order. Use one of the two types of organization above.

> goes to English classes—has no time to study
>
> works in uncle's factory—makes him tired
>
> got married in June—a lot of responsibility
>
> goes biking with his wife
>
> works evenings in gas station
>
> plays soccer with friends

 **10** Look at your notes from your interview and arrange them in the order you think you are going to write about them. Discuss the order with your partner.

Writing a Concluding Sentence

The final sentence in this kind of paragraph can summarize the paragraph or indicate some future action. The following are good concluding sentences.

> David hopes to use his new language skills to get a job in Europe this summer.
>
> All in all, Sandra thinks it has been a busy but a productive year.

These sentences are not good concluding sentences. Why not?

> Nancy has also learned to swim.
>
> Philip has moved three times this year.
>
> Ken wanted to get a job in a bakery but he couldn't find one, so he went to work in a restaurant.

11 Look at these examples of possible final sentences. Which sentence is not a good final sentence?

1. In November, Tony's wife is going to have a baby, and then he will have another thing to juggle in his busy schedule.

2. With her new English skills, Sonia is hoping to get a better job.

3. Parvin says that it's a full-time job to take care of her kids, but she can't wait till they are in school and she can get a job that pays money.

4. Chatchai has also been learning to swim.

5. Satoshi is going to return to Japan and use his English in his engineering work.

12 Write a final sentence you could use in your paragraph.

_____

_____

PART 2 | # Write

Developing Cohesion and Style

Selecting the Correct Tense

> It's important for each sentence in a paragraph about someone's life to be in the correct tense. You can use the following chart to check your verb tenses.

Verb Tenses	Notes and Examples
Simple Present	A repeated or habitual action in the present. **Example:** Mina *studies* English in Austin, Texas.
Present Continuous	An action or situation that is in progress in the present. **Example:** Mina *is studying* and *working* this quarter.
Future	An action or state that will occur in the future. **Example:** Mina *will be* in Texas for at least two years.
Past	A completed action or state. **Example:** Mina *came* to Austin three months ago.
Present Perfect	An action or, more usually, a state (with verbs like *be, have, feel, know*) that began in the past and continues in the present. Often appears with *for* and *since* + time expression. **Example:** Mina *has known* her friend Salima *since* 1996; she *has known* her friend Sally *for* one month.
Present Perfect Continuous	An action that began in the past and continues in the present; often appears with *for* and *since* + time expression. **Example:** Mina *has been working* part time in the school cafeteria since she arrived (*for* three months).

1   Complete this paragraph with the correct tenses of the verbs in parentheses. Remember that you can use the present perfect or the present perfect continuous to introduce a subject and then use the present tense to talk about it further.

This year Tony _____ (have) so much to do he _____ (feel) like a
        1   2

juggler. He _____ (get) married in June. He and his wife are very happy
              3

together but now he _____ (have) a lot more responsibility. He _____
                        4   5

(work) in his uncle's factory since April. It _____ (be) hard work, because
                                                      6

he _____ (have) to load trucks and he _____ (get) very tired. In
        7   8

addition, he _____ (work) a few evenings a week in a gas station because
                  9

he _____ (need) to save money. He also _____ (take) English
        10   11

classes at a community college near his home. He _____ (enjoy) the
                                                                12

class, but he _____ (be) so busy he _____ (not have) much time to
                  13   14

study. Tony's life _____ (not be) all work, however. In fact, he still
                        15

_____ (find) time to enjoy a few sports. He _____ (play) soccer
    16   17

with some friends every Sunday. In addition, he and his wife often _____
                                                                          18

(go) bike riding together. But she is pregnant now and _____ (have) a
                                                              19

baby in four months. Then Tony _____ (have) another thing to juggle in
                                      20

his busy schedule.

2   Write ten sentences from your interview notes. Underline each verb, then check to see if you've used the correct form.

Using Transitional Words and Phrases

However, in addition, also

The expressions *however*, *in addition*, and *also* help unify the sentences in a paragraph.

3   Find the expressions *however*, *in addition*, and *also* in the paragraph about Tony on page 128 and underline them. Then answer these questions.

1. Which two expressions do you use when you give additional information?

_____

2. Which expression do you use when you give contrasting information?

_____

3. In the paragraph about Tony, is this expression in item 2 at the beginning or end of the sentence?

_____

4. Can the expression be in another position?

_____

In fact vs. *however*

In Chapter 7, you learned to use *however* to give contrasting information. You can use *in fact* to give facts that show that the sentence before is true. Use a comma to separate *in fact* from the rest of the sentence.

Example
Tony has been very busy. *In fact*, he's been working at two jobs.

4   Add *in fact* or *however* to these sentences. Use commas where necessary.

1. Tony has been working very hard. He works from 8:00 in the morning until 9:00 at night.

_____

_____

2. Tony has been working very hard. He still finds time to play soccer every week.

_____

_____

3. Raúl has been doing well, and he likes his English class a lot. He's been studying so much that he isn't sleeping well.

_____

_____

4. Raúl has been doing well in his English class. He went from level 2 to level 4 last month.

   _____

   _____

5. Patricia enjoys going to school. She doesn't like going at night.

   _____

   _____

6. Patricia has been exercising a lot. She now runs about 30 miles a week.

   _____

   _____

5 Look at your notes and write some pairs of sentences for your paragraph. Begin the second sentence of each pair with a transitional phrase: *however, in fact, also,* or *in addition.*

_____

_____

_____

_____

Stating Results with so . . . that

> You can combine sentences giving reasons and results by using *so . . . that.*
>
> **Reason**   **Result**
> Tony has been busy.   +   He has felt like a juggler.
> Tony has been *so* busy *that* he has felt like a juggler.

6 Combine these sentences using *so . . . that.*

1. Jane has been busy. She hasn't had much time to study.

   Jane has been so busy that she hasn't had much time to study.

2. Reiko was happy. She cried.

   _____

3. Chi Wang has been working hard. He falls asleep in class.

   _____

4. Nick has been having much fun. He is seldom homesick.

    _____

5. Sonia's daughter has been sick. She had to take her to the hospital.

    _____

7 Can you write any sentences with *so . . . that* for your paragraph? Write them here.

_____

_____

_____

_____

Writing the First Draft

8 Now write your paragraph about a classmate. Use your topic sentence and notes. Also use transitional expressions to unify your paragraph.

| PART 3 | # Edit and Revise |

Editing Practice

Using Long Forms in Formal Writing

When English speakers write formally, they don't use as many contractions as when they speak—instead, they use long forms. Here are some examples of long forms and their contractions:

he has → he's	he has not → he hasn't
they have → they've	they have not → they haven't
it is → it's	it is not → it's not, it isn't

1   Write these sentences without contractions.

1. He's been playing in a band.

   <u>He has been playing in a band.</u>

2. They haven't moved yet.

   _____

3. They're not having problems with Canadian customs.

   _____

4. Recently she's been planning a party.

   _____

5. It's difficult work.

   _____

6. She's been getting dates from a computer dating service.

   _____

Spelling Present and Past Participles Correctly

2   Write the *-ing* form and the past participle of these words. The first one is done as an example. (For rules for adding *-ing*, see Appendix 1.)

	-ing Form	Past Participle
1. work	working	worked
2. begin	_____	_____
3. study	_____	_____
4. make	_____	_____
5. find	_____	_____
6. swim	_____	_____
7. go	_____	_____
8. travel	_____	_____
9. come	_____	_____
10. have	_____	_____

Using Correct Capitalization

In your paragraph, remember to capitalize words correctly. (See Appendix 2 for detailed rules.)

- ■ Capitalize months and days of the week.

  Examples

  July   September   Monday

- ■ Capitalize names of schools and businesses.

  Examples

  Lincoln Community College   Lucia's Bakery
  University of Montreal   Interspace, Inc.

- ■ Capitalize languages

  Examples

  Japanese, Spanish, Thai

3 Write these sentences with correct capitalization.

1. Pablo has been studying computer science and english at northwestern college since january.

   _____

   _____

2. Anna works as a dietician at randolph college.

   _____

3. In september Van got a job as a mail clerk at a bank.

   _____

4. Tessa has been studying fashion design every tuesday and thursday evening.

   _____

   _____

5. Irena has been working with the jones plumbing company since the fall.

   _____

   _____

4   Edit this paragraph twice and rewrite it correctly. The first time, see if the ideas are well organized. Do you need to rearrange any sentences? The second time, correct any problems with verb tenses and form. Make any other changes you think are necessary.

Marta Duarte has have a very interesting year. Last June she graduated from a tourism development course in Mexico. She received a scholarship to study English and has been attending classes here at the University of Ottawa since September. marta is twenty-five years old. She's also been traveling in Canada and the United States. She love dance and goes dancing at least two nights a week. She visits hotels to study the different management systems and has learned a lot. In fact, she says that one day in a hotel is better than ten days in a classroom. However, Marta hasn't spend all her time in Canada at work. She also find time to develop a close friendship with the manager of a big hotel here in Ottawa. She is hoping to get to know him better.

Editing Your Writing

5   Edit your paragraph using the following checklist.

> ### Editing Checklist
>
> 1. Content
>   a. Is the information interesting?
>   b. Is all the information in the paragraph important?
>
> 2. Organization
>   a. Does the topic sentence give the main idea of the paragraph?
>   b. Are the sentences well organized?
>   c. Does the paragraph have a good concluding sentence?
>
> 3. Cohesion and Style
>   a. Did you use transitional expressions correctly?
>   b. Did you use *so . . . that* correctly?
>
> 4. Grammar
>   Did you use correct verb forms?
>
> 5. Form
>   a. Did you use commas correctly?
>   b. Did you spell the verb forms correctly?
>   c. Did you use correct capitalization?

Peer Editing

6   Exchange papers with a classmate and discuss the changes you made.

Writing the Second Draft

7   Write the second draft of your paragraph using correct form. Then give it to your teacher for comments.

PART 4

A Step Beyond

Expansion Activities

1   As a class, collect all the paragraphs to make a class newsletter.

2   Recopy your paragraph without the name of the classmate you interviewed. Give your paragraph to another of your classmates. Can he or she guess who you wrote about?

3   Write a paragraph about what you have been doing in the past year. Compare the paragraph you wrote about yourself to the one that your classmate wrote about you. What are the similarities? What are the differences?

4   Write about what you and a group of people (your English class, for example) have been doing.

Journal Writing

5   Write in your journal for five minutes for a week. Then look back at your entries for the week. Write for five minutes on what you have been doing this week.

What Do You Think?

Evaluating a Day in Your Life

How do you spend your time on a typical day? Do you spend time on things you really want to do? To find out, try the following activity.

1.   Draw a large circle on a piece of paper with a pencil. Think of this circle as one day in your life.

2.   Divide your circle into four quarters using dotted lines. (Each quarter = 6 hours of the day.)

3.   Look at the questions below. Divide your circle to show about how many hours you usually spend on these items. Draw lines and label the parts of your circle as in the example. (*Important:* There is no "right" or "wrong" way to do this. Everyone's life is different!)

How many hours do you spend

■   Sleeping?

■   In school?

■   On homework?

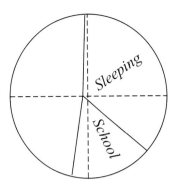

- ■ Working (if you have a job)?
- ■ Traveling (to and from school, work, etc.)?
- ■ With friends?
- ■ With family (if you are living with family)?
- ■ Alone (doing activities of your choice)?
- ■ On other activities (use your own examples)?

4. When you finish, look at your drawing. Are you happy with the way you are spending your time?

5. Draw another circle. This time, divide the circle to show how you would like to spend the day.

6. If you like, share your circle drawings with another student. Do you want to change the way you spend your time? If so, in what way(s)?

7. Write in your journal for five minutes about what you learned from this activity.

Focus on Testing

Managing Your Time

One of the greatest problems in taking an essay exam is learning to use your time wisely. For example, you should take time to plan, but if you take too much time, you won't have enough time to write. Therefore, when you take an essay exam, you should divide your time this way:

Thinking about the topic	10%
Planning and making notes	10%
Writing	70%
Revising and editing	10%

Video Activities: Online Love Story

Before You Watch.   Discuss these questions in a group.

1.   What is a "chat room?" Have you ever visited one?
2.   Do you think the Internet is a useful way to meet new people?
3.   How do you usually meet people?
4.   Do you believe that there is only one man or woman in the world who is exactly "right" for each person?

Watch.   Number the following events in the order that they happened.

_____ Patrick and Vesna chatted online.

_____ They got married.

_____ Patrick came home from work late and couldn't sleep.

_____ Patrick and Vesna got engaged.

_____ Vesna came to Patrick's house.

Watch Again.   Discuss these questions in a group.

1.   Patrick asked Vesna, "What do you look like?" Her answer was "You won't run from me." What did she mean?
2.   Why was it easy for Patrick and Vesna to meet?
3.   How soon after they met did Patrick and Vesna get engaged?
4.   How soon after that did they get married?
5.   What did Patrick and Vesna's friends predict about their relationship?
6.   What do Patrick and Vesna say about one another?
7.   What is the "Romance Network?"

After You Watch.   Work with a partner. One student is "Vesna" and the other is "Patrick." You meet in a chat room for the first time. Patrick begins by introducing himself. Then Vesna reads what he wrote and responds. Continue "chatting" until your teacher tells you to stop. You may write on paper or a computer. Be sure to ask each other questions in order to keep the conversation going.

Chapter 10

Customs, Celebrations, and Holidays

You will write a paragraph about holidays.

PART 1

Before You Write

Exploring Ideas

Describing Holidays

1   Look at the photographs and discuss them. What do you know about the holidays the people in the photos are celebrating?

2 What are the most important holidays that you celebrate? When do you celebrate these holidays? How do you celebrate them? Complete the following chart.

Holiday	Time of Year	Activities	Description of Activities

3 Work in groups. Look at your list of holidays. How could you divide them into groups? Try dividing them by seasons first (winter holidays, summer holidays). Then suggest other ways to group them (by activity, purpose, etc.).

Building Vocabulary

4 The following chart has examples of vocabulary you can use to talk about holidays. What other words did you use to describe holidays? Add your words to the list. Discuss any words you do not understand.

Nouns	Verbs	Adjectives	Other
celebration	celebrate	traditional	
commemoration	commemorate	joyous	
parade			
fireworks			
tradition			
joy			

5 In the list in Activity 4 there are some words that are part of the same word family. Word families are groups of words that have similar meanings but have different forms for different parts of speech. For example, *celebration* and *celebrate*, *tradition* and *traditional*.

There are two other pairs from the same word family. What are they?

_____ and _____

_____ and _____

1. What is the noun form of the adjective *civic*?   _____

2. What is the adjective form of the noun *independence*?   _____

3. What is the noun form of the adjective *religious*?   _____

4. What is the adjective form of the noun *importance*?   _____

5. What is the noun form of the verb *discuss*?   _____

Can you think of any other groups of words that are in the same word family?

Organizing Ideas

Categorizing and Making an Outline

Some people organize their ideas in outline form. First they write notes about their topic. Then they divide the notes into categories. Finally, they write an outline.

Here is an example of the notes that one student made about holidays in the United States.

Christmas	Independence Day	Memorial Day	Easter
New Year's	Presidents' Day	Labor Day	Passover
Thanksgiving	Valentine's Day	Halloween	Hanukkah

She decided to divide the holidays into three categories.

1. Civic holidays   2. Religious holidays   3. Traditional holidays

Before the student began to write her paragraph, she made an outline:

    I. Holidays in the United States
        A. Civic holidays
            1. Independence Day
            2. Presidents' Day
            3. Memorial Day
            4. Labor Day
        B. Traditional holidays
            1. Thanksgiving
            2. New Year's
            3. Halloween
            4. Valentine's Day
        C. Religious holidays
            1. Christian holidays
                a. Christmas
                b. Easter
            2. Jewish holidays
                a. Passover
                b. Hanukkah

6 You are going to write about holidays in one country. Choose a country, then make an outline like the one on page 142.

Ordering Information According to Importance

> When you expand an outline, you usually put the items in order of importance.

7 Here is part of an outline a student made about holidays in the United States. It shows the order of importance of traditional holidays. Can you explain why she chose this order? Notice that 1. a., 2. a., and 3. a. all have the same type of information.

     B.   Traditional holidays
         1.   Thanksgiving
             a.   Third Thursday in November
             b.   People feel thankful for the good things in their lives
             c.   Families eat turkey and other traditional foods
         2.   New Year's Day
             a.   January 1
             b.   People celebrate the New Year
         3.   Halloween
             a.   October 31
             b.   Children dress in costumes
             c.   People go to costume parties
             d.   Children collect candy

8 This student decided to write about civic holidays. She added more information to her outline, but some information is missing. Read her outline, and then read the paragraph that follows. Fill in the student's outline with the missing information.

   I.   Holidays in the United States
     A.   Civic holidays
         1.   Independence Day
             a.   Fourth of July
             b.   _____
             c.   Picnics, barbecues
             d.   Fireworks

2. _____

    a. Last weekend in May

    b. Commemorate soldiers who died in all wars

    c. Parades

    d. Put flags and flowers on graves

    e. _____

3. Labor Day

    a. _____

    b. Honor workers

    c. Parades

    d. Picnics, beach

    e. _____

4. _____

    a. _____

    b. Honor George Washington's and Abraham Lincoln's birthdays.

Holidays in the United States

There are three types of holidays: civic holidays, traditional holidays, and religious holidays. In the United States, there are more civic holidays than any other type. The most important civic holiday is Independence Day, the Fourth of July. On this day we celebrate our independence from Great Britain. Most people spend the day with their family and friends. Picnics and barbecues are very popular. In addition, almost every city and town has a fireworks display at night.

Another very important civic holiday is Memorial Day, which falls on the last weekend in May. On this holiday we commemorate all the soldiers who died for our country. Many towns and cities have parades, and some people go to cemeteries and put flowers or flags on the soldiers' graves. A third important civic holiday is Labor Day, which we celebrate on the first Monday in September. This is the day when we honor the workers of the United States. People watch parades, go on picnics, or go to the beach.

For students, Labor Day is a bittersweet holiday, because when it is over they must begin school again. Besides these three civic holidays, we also celebrate Presidents' Day on the third Monday in February. On this day we commemorate the birthdays of George Washington and Abraham Lincoln.

9   Make an outline for the type of holiday you are going to write about.

PART 2   # Write

Developing Cohesion and Style

Listing Information with in addition to, besides, another, *and* the first, second, third, last

> You can use these transitional words to add information:
>
> *in addition to, besides, another,* and *the first, second, third, last*
>
> **Examples**
> *In addition to* watching parades and going on picnics, some Americans go to the beach on Labor Day.
> *Besides* Thanksgiving and New Year's Day, there are other traditional holidays in the United States such as Halloween and Valentine's Day.
> The *first* holiday of the year is New Year's Day.

1   Look at the paragraph about holidays in the United States on page 144. Underline the transitional words that are used for adding information.

2   The following paragraphs on page 146 contain no transitional words. Complete them with the appropriate transitions. More than one answer may be correct.

Paragraph 1

Salvadorans celebrate several civic holidays each year. The most important one is Independence Day on September 15. On this day, people parade in the streets, sing songs, and recite poems. _____ important civic holiday is
₁
Labor Day. Labor Day is the first day in May. _____ Labor Day
₂
and Independence Day, Salvadorans also celebrate the birthday of José Matias Delgado, the "father of the country." ____ _____ these holidays, there
₃
are other minor holidays such as *Dia de la Raza*.

Paragraph 2

There are some traditional holidays in the United States that no one celebrates seriously. The _____ one is
₄
Ground Hog Day. Ground Hog Day is February 2. On this day, people look for ground hogs coming out of their nests in the ground. Traditional belief says that if the ground hog sees his shadow, there will be six more weeks of winter.

_____ silly holiday is April
₅
Fool's Day. This holiday falls on April first. On this day, people play tricks on

A groundhog

each other. _____ Ground Hog Day and April Fools Day, there is
₆
Sadie Hawkins Day. Sadie Hawkins Day is on November 13th. On this day, tradition says that women can ask men to marry them.

Unifying a Paragraph with Pronouns and Pronominal Expressions

You can use pronouns to refer to things you have already mentioned so that you don't have to repeat the same words again and again.

3 Here is a list of the pronouns and pronominal expressions in the paragraph about holidays in the United States on pages 144–145. Tell what each one refers to.

1. on this day (line 4) _____Independence Day_____

2. on this holiday (line 8) _____

3. this is the day (line 12) _____

4. it (line 14) _____

5. they (line 14) _____

6. these three civic holidays (line 15) _____

4 The paragraph that follows needs more pronouns. Edit it and substitute pronouns or pronominal expressions for *some* of the nouns. Remember that too many pronouns are as bad as too few.

Americans celebrate several traditional holidays. One traditional holiday Americans celebrate is New Year's. In fact, New Year's is the first holiday of the year. Many people often go to parties on New Year's Eve. In addition, on New Year's Eve, Americans sometimes wear silly hats and blow horns. At midnight, Americans kiss the people near them and wish everyone a Happy New Year at New Year's Eve parties.

Using Quantifiers

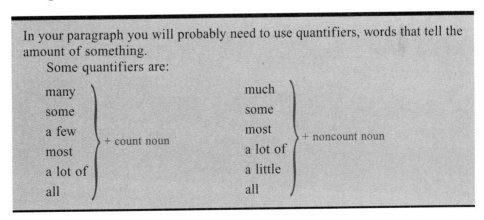

In your paragraph you will probably need to use quantifiers, words that tell the amount of something.
Some quantifiers are:

| many
some
a few
most
a lot of
all } + count noun | much
some
most
a lot of
a little
all } + noncount noun |

5 How many quantifiers can you find in the paragraph about holidays in the United States? Underline them.

Using Nonrestrictive Relative Clauses

> ■ In Chapter 7 you learned about restrictive relative clauses with *who* and *that*. A restrictive relative clause tells you which person or thing the writer is referring to.
>
> **Examples**
>
> Christmas is the Christian holiday *that* children like best.
>
> Children *who* have been good get many presents on this day.
>
> ■ A nonrestrictive relative clause gives additional information. In nonrestrictive clauses, use *which* instead of *that*. Use commas to separate a nonrestrictive clause from the rest of the sentence.
>
> **Examples**
>
> Thanksgiving, *which falls in November,* is a time for families.
>
> Another traditional holiday is Halloween, *which is mainly for children.*
>
> ■ The information in a nonrestrictive relative clause is not necessary. You can omit a nonrestrictive relative clause, but you cannot omit a restrictive relative clause.
>
> **Examples**
>
> Thanksgiving, *which falls in November,* is a time for families to get together. (nonrestrictive)
>
> Notice that you can omit the clause *which falls in November*: Thanksgiving is a time for families to get together.
>
> Christmas is the holiday *that I like best.* (restrictive)
>
> Notice that if you omit the clause *that I like best*, the sentence is incomplete: Christmas is the holiday.

6 Combine these sentences with *which* and a nonrestrictive relative clause. Insert a clause at the ^ mark.

1. Easter‸is a happy holiday. Easter comes in the springtime.

    Easter, which comes in the springtime, is a happy holiday.
    _____

2. The Fourth of July‸is a time for big parades and fireworks. The Fourth of July is Independence Day.

    _____

    _____

3. Martin Luther King Day‸comes in January. Martin Luther King Day is our newest holiday.

    _____

    _____

4. Halloween∧is a favorite children's holiday. Halloween is an ancient British
    tradition.

    _____

5. On New Year's Day∧there is a famous parade in Pasadena, California. New
    Year's Day is the first holiday of the year.

    _____

    _____

6. Ground Hog Day∧is not a serious holiday. Ground Hog Day is in February.

    _____

7. Songkran∧is in April. Songkran is Thai New Years.

    _____

8. My town∧has a famous parade on Independence Day. My town is very
    small.

    _____

9. Chinese New Year∧lasts for several days, Chinese New Year is in February.

    _____

10. Arbor Day and Flag Day∧are in April and June. Arbor Day and Flag Day
    are not famous holidays.

    _____

    _____

7 Write three sentences using nonrestrictive relative clauses about the holiday in your
outline. Use correct punctuation.

_____

_____

_____

_____

_____

What Do You Think?

Examining the Meaning of Holidays

Holiday celebrations are so common that most people do not question why we have holidays. In small groups discuss the following.

1. What are some different purposes of holidays that you celebrate?
2. Are some holidays more special or important to some people (or groups of people) than to others? Why?
3. Are there any holidays that used to be important but aren't now? Why?

Writing the First Draft

8 Write your paragraph about holidays in the country you have chosen. Use your outline and the sentences you wrote using nonrestrictive relative clauses.

PART 3   # Edit and Revise

Editing Practice

Punctuating Nonrestrictive Relative Clauses

■ Use commas to separate a nonrestrictive clause from the rest of the sentence. If the clause comes in the middle of the sentence, use two commas.

Example

Valentine's Day, which falls on February 14, is a holiday for sweethearts.

■ If the clause comes at the end of the sentence, use only one comma.

Example

Memorial Day is in May, which is almost the beginning of the summer in the United States.

1   Add commas where necessary in these sentences.

1. Songkran which is the Thai New Year is on April 13.

2. Eid-e-Ghorbon is a religious holiday in Iran which is a Muslim country.

3. Christmas which is an important holiday in Christian countries is usually a happy time.

4. Bastille Day which is on July 14 is a very important holiday in France.

5. My birthday which is February 24th is a holiday in Mexico.

6. Labor Day is the first weekend in September which is also the beginning of school in the United States.

7. Day of the Dead which is an important holiday in many Christian countries is not celebrated in the United States.

8. Groundhog Day which Americans celebrate on February 2nd is not an official holiday.

2   Edit the paragraph entitled "Traditional Holidays in the United States" and rewrite it correctly. The first time, check to see if the order of ideas is correct. (See the outline on page 143 if you need help.) The second time, check to see if the writer has used quantifiers correctly. Make any other changes you think are necessary. When you are finished, exchange papers with another student and look at his/her changes. Discuss the differences.

Traditional Holidays in the United States

There are four important traditional holidays in the United States. Another important traditional holiday is New Year's. On New Year's Eve, most people go to parties. At twelve o'clock, everyone shouts "Happy New Year!" and they wish their friends good luck. New Year's parties usually last a long time. Some people don't go home until morning. The most important of these holidays is Thanksgiving, which we celebrate on the third Thursday in November. This is a family holiday. Most of people spend the day with their

relatives. They feel thankful for the good things in their lives. The most important tradition on this day is Thanksgiving dinner. At a traditional Thanksgiving dinner, the most people eat turkey with stuffing, cranberry sauce, and pumpkin pie. The third traditional holiday, Halloween, is mainly for children. On this holiday, people dress as witches, ghosts, or other such things. Much children go from house to house and say "Trick or treat." If the people at the house do not give them candy, the children will play a trick on them; but, this hardly ever happens. A most give them candy or fruit. Another holiday is Valentine's Day, which is in February. On this day, people give each other cards, flowers, or candy.

Editing Your Writing

3 Edit your paragraph using the following checklist.

Editing Checklist

1. Content
   a. Is the information interesting?
   b. Is there enough information?

2. Organization
   a. Did you list the holidays from most important to least important?
   b. Did you give the same type of information about each holiday?

3. Cohesion and Style
   a. Did you use expressions such as *in addition to, besides, another, the first (second,* etc.)?
   b. Did you use quantifiers correctly?
   c. Did you use pronouns and pronominal expressions appropriately?
   d. Did you use relative clauses correctly?

Peer Editing

4 Exchange papers with a classmate and discuss the changes you made.

Writing the Second Draft

5 Write the second draft of your paragraph using correct form. Then give it to your teacher for comments.

| PART 4 | # A Step Beyond |

Expansion Activities

1 Bring in pictures to illustrate different holidays that your class celebrates. Write captions and put the pictures on a bulletin board.

2 Make a book about holidays. Use pictures and writing to explain the holidays that you celebrate. Share your book with your classmates.

3 Write a paragraph about your favorite holiday.

4 Interview a classmate about her or his favorite holiday. In a paragraph, explain why it is her or his favorite.

Journal Writing

5 In your journal, write about how you feel about holidays now compared with how you felt when you were younger.

Focus on Testing

Organizing Your Ideas

When taking an essay exam, it is important to organize your ideas before you write. This will make your paragraph flow more smoothly. The following steps can help you organize your writing.

1. Read the topic carefully.
2. Make notes on the different points you want to write about.
3. Organize your notes. Group similar points together. Number the points (or groups of points) from the most important to the least important.
4. Check to make sure that all your points relate to the topic; delete any points that don't.
5. Write your paragraph using your organized notes.

Timed Activity: 15 Minutes

To practice this skill, choose one of the topics below. Then make notes on the topic. Finally group the ideas that belong together and decide the order that you are going to present them in.

Being an Only Child/the Eldest/Youngest Child Is a Challenge

The Importance of Good Nutrition

Why I Like Living in the City (or Country)

Video Activities: Puerto Rican Day Parade

Before You Watch.   Discuss these questions in a group.

1. What is a parade?

2. What kinds of things and people can you see in a parade?

3. What do you know about Puerto Rico?

Watch.   Discuss these questions in a group.

1. What does the Puerto Rican Day Parade commemorate?

2. Which of the following things or people were part of the parade?

spectators	a marching band	floats
a fire truck	clowns	police
a queen	flag wavers	the mayor of New York

Watch Again.   Fill in the missing information.

1. Columbus discovered Puerto Rico _____ years ago.

2. The queen says she feels _____ of her people.

3. The kind of music that Tito Puente plays is called _____.

4. _____ people traveled from Puerto Rico to New York for the parade.

After You Watch.   Write a paragraph about a parade you have seen. You may include some or all of the following information or add other facts:

The name of the parade

When and where you saw it

The weather, feeling, or atmosphere of the parade

How many spectators there were

Who walked or rode in the parade (people, entertainment, floats, etc.)

Why you will always remember this day

Chapter 11

Science and Technology

IN THIS CHAPTER

You will write a message to a computer discussion group about control of electronic communication.

PART 1	# Before You Write

Exploring Ideas

Discussing Computer Networks and Newsgroups

 1 Read the following article. Then discuss the questions near the end of the article in small groups.

The Information Superhighway

In recent years, there has been a revolution in communication that has connected people all over the world. You can now sit at your desk, make a telephone call from your computer, and connect to a network that will allow you to explore information in computers from Acapulco to Zhenjiang.

You can find out soccer scores for your hometown team, shop for the latest computer equipment, have an electronic "chat" with other people about your favorite movie star, read and post articles on the latest international crisis, or play chess with a team of international players. You can use search engines to look for information stored in computers all over the world. In thousands of computer discussion groups you can read and send messages on almost any subject—some of which you wouldn't want your children to see. You can even play your favorite music and send photographs to your friends and family.

The network with the most information is the Internet (or "Net"). The Net started as a way for scientists and computer experts to communicate and share information. Universities, research groups, and governments paid for it, and only people with advanced computer knowledge could use it. Now almost anyone can access the Internet, and they can send or receive almost any kind of information. This freedom of access can be good or bad, and there are many unanswered questions about it, such as:

- Should governments, or any other group, try to control the Internet?
- What role should advertising play on the Net?
- Should the Internet carry *any* kind of communication? What about censoring criminal activity, racist messages, or sex discussions or pictures?
- Should people be allowed to "flame" (verbally attack) *anyone* or *any* subject?
- Should people be able to control the amount of "spam" (electronic junk mail) sent to their E-mail address?

These questions of freedom versus control will never be answered to everyone's satisfaction, and they will probably be the subject of interesting discussions for a long time.

Building Vocabulary

2   This chart has examples of terms commonly used in computer networking. Add other
words you used in your discussion to the list. Then choose the correct terms from the
list to complete sentences 1 to 6 that follow the chart.

Nouns	Verbs	Other
network	network	_____
chat room	censor	_____
e-mail	download	_____
censorship	upload	_____
spam	flame	_____
electronic	access	_____
search engine	e-mail	_____
_____	_____	_____
_____	_____	_____
_____	_____	_____

1. When you want to send a message you have already written to a discussion
    group, you can _____ it to the group in only a few seconds.

2. An electronic _____ is a group of computers connected
    together to communicate and share information.

3. By using a _____, you can search for information on any
    subject on the Web.

4. When you connect to the Internet, you have _____ to
    computers around the world.

5. You can _____ a message from a newsgroup to save it on
    your computer.

6. People on the Internet do not agree on how to _____ illegal
    activity.

Organizing Ideas

Organizing an E-mail Message to a Discussion Group

You are going to write a message to a computer discussion group on the topic of censorship. In your message, you will give your opinion about one of the four questions in the article you just read.

Messages to discussion groups are generally organized like other writing, with a few minor differences. Here are a few special rules for organizing E-mail messages. Many of these "rules" have developed informally and are referred to as "netiquette." (*Netiquette* is a combination of the words *network* and *etiquette;* the word *etiquette* means "a set of rules for good behavior.")

Internet Netiquette

- Because so many messages are sent to computer newsgroups, keep your message short.

- Keep to the topic of the discussion group. People will get angry if you don't!

- Keep your message simple and informal. Discussion groups are for ordinary people. Don't try to use big words and difficult sentences.

- If you are responding to another message, quote a few lines from the message so people who didn't read it know what you are talking about.

- Give your main idea in a few sentences so people can quote a few lines from your message when they reply to it.

- People on the Internet express their opinions strongly, and you can find some very strong personal attacks on the Net. Express your opinion strongly, but don't call people names or attack them personally when you disagree with them.

- Don't only criticize other messages—offer positive suggestions.

- Don't type in all capital letters. On computer networks, this means you are angry and are SHOUTING.

---

3   Read these two messages from the newsgroup on censorship. Each one contains information that is not on the subject of computer network censorship. Find that information and cross it out.

Topic: Ban Advertising on the Internet
Written 10:10 am Jan 5 by lmbewe@dlu.edu
***Advertising ruins our cities, our highways, our magazines, and our TV. Every night I have to throw away dozens of pieces of junk mail I receive that advertise products I don't want. The U.S. mail system has gotten so bad that I don't receive mail I need, only stupid advertisements. Now the same thing is happening to the Internet! Everyday I receive e mail advertisements from companies I have never heard of. Can't there be at least one place where human beings can communicate without some people trying to make money off us?
Lionel Mbewe
lmbewe@dlu.edu

The second message is a response to Lionel. Note that when some Net users sign their name, they may also include their regular address and/or one of their favorite quotations.

Written 8:32pm Jan 7 by freebie@freepr.mrfs.qu.ca
>Can't there be at least one place where human beings can communicate without some people trying to make money off us?
It would be nice, but let's be real: it would be impossible to keep advertising out of the Internet. In fact, it is already here, in special discussion groups that share information about different products. One of the freedoms that we have is the freedom to make money, as long as the making of money does not break some other law. We have to make realistic rules to control advertising on the Net, not to ban it completely. Why don't all the people involved in this question--companies who want to advertise, ordinary people against advertising, the groups that provide access to the Net, and experienced users--get together on-line and seriously work toward setting controls on advertising? Right now it's just talk, talk, and more talk!
So many people who send messages to the Internet are scientists and university researchers who live far away from the real lives of most of us who need to make money. They don't need to advertise on the Internet--they have good safe jobs. University professors should be required to spend time outside in the real world before they go into the classroom and try to tell us ordinary people the way it is.
Cindy McPherson, People's Free Press, 7592 rue Berri, Montreal, Quebec, H2J 2R6, Canada freebie@freepr.mrfs.on.ca
"None can love freedom heartily, but good men--the rest love not freedom, but license.- John Milton

4 In groups, discuss what you crossed out in Activity 3 and why it doesn't belong.

5 Cindy quoted the lines she thought gave the main idea of Lionel's message. What lines would you quote as the main idea of Cindy's message? What positive suggestion did Cindy give?

6 Choose one of the five questions in the article on page 156. Write two or three sentences that give your opinion about the question. Offer positive suggestions if possible and make sure you are writing only about that topic. If you want to respond to one of the preceding messages, mark the sentences that you will quote to give the main idea of the message you are responding to.

Supporting Your Opinion

> While your E-mail message should be short, it should include support for your opinion. That is, you need to give examples or reasons that illustrate your point of view or prove your argument.

7 In her reply to Lionel, Cindy wrote that it would be impossible to keep advertising out of the Internet. She gave one supporting example and one supporting reason. What are they?

Supporting example: _____

_____

Supporting reason: _____

_____

8 Read the newsgroup message below. The writer first quotes another message and then gives his opinion. Find the writer's opinion and underline it.

Written 11:25 am Mar 17 by mjanovic@comp.usc.ca.us
> Words cannot hurt anyone. Any censorship, no matter how well-meaning, will in the >end be used to prevent people from speaking their mind. The Internet, now a wild and >wonderful place, will become just another piece of media controlled by people with >money.

I don't understand how anybody can argue for total freedom from censorship on the Internet. I can only think that they don't have children. I have two daughters, aged 10 and 14. They see me using the Internet and are anxious to learn how. And I'm anxious for them to get involved. However, I don't let them have access when I'm not around. There are controls on sex and violence in other media: why not on the Internet?

Mike Janovic mjanovic@comp.usc.ca.us

---

9 In small groups, discuss what examples or reasons Mike could give to support his opinion by answering the following questions. Write your answers on the lines below.

1. Why would a parent be anxious for her or his children to get involved in the Internet?

   _____

   _____

2. Why wouldn't a parent want his or her children to have access to the Internet when he or she is not around?

   _____

   _____

10 Look at the sentences you wrote in Activity 6 giving your opinion about one of the five questions in the article on page 156. Write each sentence again. Under each sentence, give reasons and examples supporting your opinion.

Writing E-mail Topic Lines

E-mail messages don't include titles. Instead, the topic is written after the word *Topic:,* which appears on the computer screen. This topic is just like a title: It should give the main idea of your message and make people want to read it. The topic is included in the index of messages, which people use to decide which messages to read, so it is important. When writing your topic, follow the same rules of capitalization as you do for titles.

11   Write a topic for the message on page 161 from Mike Janovic.

   Topic: _____

   _____

12   Write a topic for the message you are going to write.

   Topic: _____

   _____

PART 2   # Write

Developing Cohesion and Style

Unifying Your Writing with Synonyms and Pronouns

> One way of unifying your writing is to refer to the same word or topic several times. However, a paragraph doesn't flow smoothly if you often repeat the same word in phrases that are near each other. To refer to a word or topic in a nearby phrase, you should use:
>
> ■ pronouns such as *it*, *they*, *this*, and *these*, or
>
> ■ synonyms (words with the same or similar meaning), often used with *this* or *these*
>
> If you haven't used a word in a few sentences, then you can repeat it.

1   Look at the third paragraph in the article on page 156 about the Internet. Find and underline the pronoun *it* and the synonym *the Net* where these terms are used to refer to the Internet. Note that the word *Internet* is repeated a few times also.

2   Look at this list of words with similar meanings. Insert the appropriate words in the sentences that follow.

   computer (used as adj)—electronic
   censor—control (v)
   access (v)—connect to
   criminal (used as adj)—illegal

The Internet is a huge computer network. People connected to the Net can

participate in _____ discussions called bulletin boards. Because so
₁

many people can now _____ these bulletin boards, the question of
₂

who should control information on the Internet is an important topic for

discussion. For example, should the government try to _____ the
₃

Internet for racist messages or _____ activity?
₄

Language for Giving Opinions and Suggestions

There are phrases you can use to give polite opinions; there are also suggestions and phrases you should avoid if you want to be polite. Use *should, need to, it would be better if,* or *why don't/doesn't* instead of *must.*

Examples

The Internet *should* censor messages for racist language.

Why doesn't the Internet censor messages for racist language?

The Internet *needs to* censor messages for racist language.

It would be better if the Internet censored messages for racist language.

3   Find the language Cindy and Lionel used on page 159 to give opinions and suggest ways they can make their messages more polite.

4   Look at the opinions and suggestions you wrote earlier in the chapter. Have you expressed them politely?

Writing the First Draft

5   Using the opinions and supporting reasons and examples you have written, write your E-mail message. Make sure you state your main idea somewhere in your message and support your opinion with reasons and/or examples. First write a topic line, your message (quoting another message if you like), and then your name and electronic address. If you don't have an electronic address, write your first initial and last name, the "@" symbol, the initials of your school, a period, and then "edu," as in the following example:

blelieu@und.edu

What Do You Think?

Considering Personal Privacy in the Workplace

Today many companies tell their employees that they can use their computers and electronic networks—including E-mail—for company work only; they cannot use them for any personal (non-business) purpose. Furthermore, companies say they have the right to read the content of employee's electronic messages without their permission. Employees who are found using computers or E-mail for nonbusiness purposes may lose their jobs. What do you think of such a business policy? Do you think a company has the right to read its employees' E-mail without asking their permission? Should an employee lose his or her job over using E-mail for a nonbusiness purpose, such as sending an E-mail message to a friend?

PART 3   # Edit and Revise

Editing Practice

Spelling and Grammar in Computer Messages

> Luckily for non-native speakers of English, one of the netiquette rules is not to flame people for grammar or spelling mistakes. Of course, you should use correct grammar and spelling so your message is clear and easy to read. (If someone does flame you, you might write back asking how well they would communicate in your native language!) If you are writing on a computer, use a computer spell-check program.

1 Edit this reply to Mike Janovic, who wanted censorship in the Internet. First omit any personal attacks or lines that aren't on the topic. Then add support to the opinion expressed and/or give a positive suggestion. Finally, use pronouns and/or synonyms in place of the word *Internet* and correct spelling and grammar. (Note that since you can't underline on the Internet, writers use asterisks ** instead.)

Response 1 of 1

>I don't understand how anybody can argue for total freedom from censorship on the Internet. . . . There are controls on sex and violence in other media: why not on the Internet?

>That's just the point: the Internet is *not* like all other media. It is selfish peabrains like Mr. Janovic who one day ruin the Internet. The Internet not for childs, the Internet for adults. If peple want a Sesame Street Internet, they should make there own Internet and not ruining our Internet. Childs must to be controled. Parents let them run wild in the street. They taking drugs and killing peple.

Editing Your Writing

2   Edit your message using the following checklist.

Editing Checklist

1. Content
   a. Does the message express your opinion strongly without personal attacks?
   b. Have you given reasons and examples to support your opinions?
2. Organization
   a. Are all your sentences on the topic of the discussion group?
   b. Does your message contain a sentence or two that gives the main idea of your message?
   c. Does your topic line give the main idea of your message and make people want to read it?
3. Cohesion and Style
   a. Does your message use pronouns and synonyms to unify your writing?
   b. Have you used polite phrases to give opinions and suggestions?
4. Grammar
   a. Are your verbs correct?
   b. Have you used correct grammatical forms to give opinions and suggestions?
5. Form
   a. Have you avoided writing in all capitals?
   b. Have you capitalized the important words in your topic line correctly?
   c. Have you put front brackets before lines quoting other messages?
   d. Have you written a signature under your message with your name and electronic address?

Peer Editing

3   Give your message to another student to check.

Writing the Second Draft

4   Rewrite your message using correct form. Then give it to your teacher for comments.

PART 4   # A Step Beyond

Expansion Activities

1   If possible, send your messages. Find a newsgroup topic, send your message, and see what replies you receive. If you don't have access to a computer bulletin board, you can use a regular bulletin board. Post your messages on the board, and students from your class or another class can read the messages and respond to them.

2   Look at this list of discussion group "addresses" and descriptions. When you participate in discussion groups, you can look at an index of messages that people post and choose which ones to read. You can download the most interesting ones onto your computer to read later, and you can upload messages of your own. Which discussion groups would you be interested in reading? Which ones would you like to write about? What would you write? Would you like to visit or start a newsgroup on another topic? What would the subject be?

alt.shy.support	A discussion by and about shy people.
biz.ad.internet	A discussion about advertising on the Internet.
tes1.1	Questions and answers about teaching English as a second language.
comp.support.com	Questions and answers about problems with communications software.
rec.soccer.intl	A discussion about international soccer/football.
soc.immigra	A discussion about immigration in America.
alt.best.of.internet	A place where people post their favorite messages.

3   Print out some of your favorite discussion group messages. Read or duplicate them so your classmates can respond to them.

Journal Writing

4   The following activity is called a free association activity. Choose one of the topics
below. As quickly as possible, write down all the words you associate with that topic.
Don't censor or omit any word you think of, no matter how silly or unrelated to the
subject it seems. (Write the words in your native language if you don't know them
in English.) Then write your opinion of the topic using some of the words from your
free-association practice.

1. Computers
2. Advertising
3. The English language
4. Writing
5. Your home

Focus on Testing

Making an Outline of Supporting Examples and Reasons

On essay tests that require you to express your opinion about a topic, it's very
important to include supporting examples and reasons. An outline can help you
organize your ideas quickly. Write your opinion(s), leaving space for supporting
examples and reasons. Then ask the question "why?" to think of supporting
examples and reasons and note them on your outline. You can then be sure that
you have supported each opinion with reasons and examples.

Timed Activity: 8 Minutes
Choose one of the following topics. Decide if you agree or not. Brainstorm
supporting arguments and reasons for your opinion. Then share your work with
a classmate. Does he or she think that you have listed good reasons? Does he or
she think that your examples support your reasons?

1. Access to the Internet should be free for everyone.
2. Children should only use the Internet under adult supervision.
3. The Internet is helping people build relationships.
4. The Internet is antisocial.

Video Activities: Sight for the Blind

Before You Watch. Discuss the following questions with your class or in a small group.

1. How can technology help physically challenged people? Give examples.
2. As a child, did you ever try to "pretend" you were blind (unable to see)? How did it feel?

Watch. Write answers to these questions.

1. Who is Jerry, and who is Craig? _____

   _____

2. How does the new technology help Jerry? _____

   _____

3. Jerry is _____ years old. He became blind _____ years ago.
4. Craig has been blind for _____ year(s).

Watch Again. Circle the correct answers.

1. Craig became blind

   a. at birth   b. in an accident   c. because of a disease

2. According to Craig, when people pretend to be blind, they always cheat. He means:

   a. They ask someone to help them.
   b. They never really close their eyes.
   c. They open their eyes just a little.

3. The new device that helps Jerry to see uses a

   a. camera   b. computer   c. transistor

4. Craig's biggest dream is to _____ again.
5. How does Craig feel about the future?

   a. sad   b. hopeful   c. worried

After You Watch. Write a short composition on one of the following.

1. How else can technology help people overcome challenges or do things that are very difficult? For example, how do voice-activated machines help people?
2. Describe how someone can overcome a physical challenge or do something that is very difficult.

Chapter 12

The Global Consumer

IN THIS CHAPTER

You will write a letter of complaint about something you bought that you are dissatisfied with.

PART 1

Before You Write

Exploring Ideas

Discussing Consumer Problems and Complaints

1   Look at the following pictures, which show people who have just bought something that they are not happy with. What's wrong in each picture?

2   Discuss these questions in small groups.

1.   Have you ever bought something from a store and been disappointed with it? What was the item? What was wrong with it?
2.   What did you do? Did you keep the item? Did you write a letter to complain? Did you take it back? If you took it back, what happened?

Building Vocabulary

3   This chart has examples of vocabulary commonly used in talking about consumer problems and complaints. Add other words you used in your discussion to the list. Discuss any words you do not understand.

Nouns	Verbs	Adjectives	Other
refund	refund	defective	_____
receipt	exchange	dissatisfied	_____
guarantee	return	guaranteed	_____
warranty	complain	_____	_____
complaint department	purchase	_____	_____
manager	_____	_____	_____
_____	_____	_____	_____
_____	_____	_____	_____

Organizing Ideas

Writing an Effective Letter of Complaint

A well-written letter of complaint should:

1. Be addressed to a person who can do something about the problem.
2. Be polite.
3. State the problem clearly and simply.
4. Give definite details that explain *who* did *what, when, where,* and *why.*
5. Include receipts, order numbers, prices, and other important details if available.
6. Suggest a solution.

4   Read the letter below. Find examples of the points above.

Mr. David Chen
Customer Service Manager
Northstar Computer Company
12 King Street
Singapore

Dear Mr. Chen,

    I recently bought a Northstar 800 computer from your catalog. I am sorry to tell you that I am very disappointed in it. Although the catalog says that it is easy to use, I have been unable to even connect it. I have called your service representatives several times but they have not been helpful. I have had this computer for two weeks and feel totally frustrated. I have all the boxes and packing materials. I would like to return the computer to you for a refund of the purchase price ($850.00). I will gladly pay the shipping cost if you agree to reimbursement for the total cost of the computer.

    Thank you for your prompt attention to this matter.

Sincerely,

Kenneth Liu

5   Jaime Flores bought a kitchen appliance from a mail order catalog. Read his letter of complaint. Where does he need to add details?

> Dear Sir or Madam,
>
>   The other day I ordered an electric frying pan from your catalog. When it arrived, it didn't work. Please refund my money.
>
>   Sincerely,
>
>   *Jaime Flores*
>   Jaime Flores

6   Marie Wolpert bought a suitcase at a large department store. She is unhappy with it and would like to return it. Here are notes for a letter that she is writing to the department manager. Read them and draw a line through any unnecessary details.

1. Skyway suitcase
2. 300" x 450"
3. light blue
4. purchased June 17
5. paid cash
6. reduced from $50 to $42
7. handle broke on trip to Buffalo
8. handle broke first time used
9. called the store
10. spoke with the manager of luggage department on July 15
11. manager said no refunds or exchanges on sale items
12. manager's name Simon Grey
13. would like to exchange suitcase

7   Think of something you bought that you were dissatisfied with. Make a list of the important details. (If you can't remember all the details, you can write what you think might have happened.)

_____

_____

_____

_____

_____

_____

8 Exchange lists with another student in your class. Can you understand the situation? Has he or she included all the important information? Has he or she included any unnecessary details? Ask your partner any information that you can't understand or ask him/her to tell you what happened.

PART 2	# Write

Developing Cohesion and Style

Using Past Participles as Adjectives

> The past participle of a verb can also function as an adjective. For example, the past participle *broken* functions as part of the present perfect tense in the following sentence:
>
> > Oh no! I have *broken* the bowl!
>
> However, in this sentence, broken functions as an adjective:
>
> > When the bowl arrived, it was *broken*.

1 Look at these verbs and write their past participles. Then use the past participles as adjectives in a sentence.

Example

stain   *stained*

The blouse is stained with tomato juice.

1. smash   _____

   _____

2. crack   _____

   _____

3. destroy   _____

   _____

4. tear   _____

   _____

5. fade   _____

_____

6. lose   _____

_____

7. rip   _____

_____

8. scratch   _____

_____

9. chip   _____

_____

10. break   _____

_____

2 Look at the notes you made in Activity 2 in Part 1 about something you bought that you were dissatisfied with. Write five sentences about your complaint using past participles as adjectives.

Using Formal Language

A business letter should be formal and polite. To make a business letter polite, you shouldn't be too direct. Generally, the fewer words you use at the beginning of a complaint or request, the more direct and less polite it is. To make a request more polite, add polite words or phrases to the beginning of the sentence:

Less Polite: Refund my money.

Please refund my money.

Would (Could) you please refund my money?

More Polite: I would appreciate it if you would refund my money.

3 Look at the following letter of complaint. Rewrite it to make it more formal and more polite.

> Dear Sir or Madam,
>
>   Last week I bought a set of six glasses in your store. You sent them to my home. When I got the package, four of the glasses were broken. I want a refund for all six glasses. Send it to me soon.
>
>   Sincerely,
>
>   *Kate Collins*
>
>   Kate Collins

_____

_____

_____

_____

_____

_____

_____

Writing the First Draft

4 Write the first draft of your letter of complaint. Use your notes and the sentences you wrote using past participles and adjectives. Remember to include all important details without adding unnecessary information. Also add polite expressions to any requests you make.

PART 3 # Edit and Revise

Editing Practice

Following the Format of a Business Letter

1 Look at the following business letter. It shows one correct format for a business letter. (There are several correct formats.) Then do Activity 2 on page 178.

Heading {
15 South Cedar Street

Boston, Massachusetts 02214

January 11, 20XX
}

Manager

Sales Department

Universal Publishing Company   } Inside Address

1523 Castleton Boulevard

New York, New York 10027

Dear Sir or Madam: Salutation

     On December 15, 20XX I ordered one copy of "The
United States in Pictures" by Jerome Massanti. I
included a check for the full price of the book, $18.97
plus $2.00 for shipping and handling charges. On
December 27 of last year, I received a letter from your
order department that said that the book would not be
available until May of this year. The letter also said
that if I wanted a refund, I could have it. On January
2, I wrote and asked them to refund my $20.97. It is
now four weeks later, and I still have not received my
refund.

     Would you please look into this matter for me? I
have often ordered books from your company and
would like to continue doing business with you.

Closing   Very truly yours,

Signature   *Simon La Grande*

Simon La Grande

Body

A business letter should contain all the following elements:

Heading   The heading gives the writer's address and the date. It should be in the upper right-hand corner of the first page, an inch or more from the top. The address should include:

- number and street or post office box number
- city, state or province, postal code
- country (if the letter is sent out of the country)

Inside Address   The inside address contains the name and the address of the person or company you are writing to. It is usually on the left, two spaces below the date. If you know the name and title of the person, you should include them. For example:

David Pearson, Manager

Sales Department

Margaret McGraw, Customer Relations

Salutation   The salutation or greeting should be two spaces below the inside address. The most common salutations are:

Dear Sir or Madam:

Dear Mr. Frasier:

Dear Ms. Kaplan:

Dear Mrs. Foster:

Body   The body of the letter begins two spaces below the salutation. You should indent the paragraphs. There should be a margin of at least one inch on both sides of the paper, at the top, and at the bottom. If your letter is very short, you should make your margins larger.

Closing and Signature   The closing is two spaces below the last line of the body. A comma follows it. Capitalize only the first word. Some common ways to close formal letters are:

Very truly yours,

Yours truly,

Sincerely,

Sincerely yours,

Sign the letter about one-half inch below the closing. Then type or print your name under your signature.

2 Put the following information into the correct place in the letter form below it. Add commas where necessary.

Customer Service Department, Sullivan Office Furniture
Company, 1432 Bradley Boulevard, Muskegon, Michigan 49441
July 12, 20XX
Dear Sir or Madam:
157 John Street, New York, New York 10038
Yours sincerely
Jane Fulton
Jane Fulton
Office Manager

_____

_____

_____

_____

_____

_____

_____

      XXXXXXXXXXXXXXXXXXXXXXXXXXXXXXXXXXXXXXXXXXXXX
XXXXXXXXXXXXXXXXXXXXXXXXXXXXXXXXXXXXXXXXXXXXX
XXXXXXXXXXXXXXXXXXXXXXXXXXXXXXXXXXXXXXXXXXXXX
XXXXXXXXXXXXXXXXXXXXXXXXXXXXXXXXXXXXXXXXXXXXX
    XXXXXXXXXXXXXXXXXXXXXXXXXXXXXXXXXXXXXXXXXXXXX
XXXXXXXXXXXXXXXXXXXXXXXXXXXXXXXXXXXXXXXXXXXXX

_____

_____

_____

3   Edit this letter twice and rewrite it correctly. The first time, check to see if the writer has used correct business letter form. Then check to see if the writer included all the necessary details, if he should take out some of the details, and if he has used polite, formal language. Make any other changes you think are necessary.

February 24, 20XX

125 South Street
Brattleboro
Vermont 05301

David Drew
Manager Service Dept.
National Electronics Company
309 Fourth St.
Pipe Creek, Texas 78063

dear manager

last month I sent my CD player to you for repairs because it wasn't working correctly. I got it for my birthday. You service department promise to send to me in two weeks. I still haven't gotten it back. I need my CD player now. You had better tell them to repair it and send it to me quickly.

David Wright

Editing Your Writing

4   Edit your letter using the following checklist.

Editing Checklist

1. Content
    Did you explain the problem clearly?
2. Organization
    a. Did you include all the necessary details?
    b. Did you include any unnecessary details?
3. Cohesion and Style
    a. Did you use formal language?
    b. Did you use polite language?
4. Grammar
    a. Did you use correct verb forms?
    b. Did you use past participles as adjectives correctly?
5. Form
    Did you use the correct business letter format, with a date, inside address, salutation, and closing?

Peer Editing

5 Exchange letters with another student. Discuss the letters. Are there any other changes you should make?

Focus on Testing

Evaluating Supporting Details

When judging essay tests, teachers often look for arguments with appropriate and effective supporting details. Essays should include important details to support an argument and not include unnecessary details, just like a letter of complaint.

    Look at the list of details you just wrote. How effective do you think they will be in supporting the argument you are making? Are there details you could add or change to make the person you are writing to more likely to respond to your request? Since you are probably writing about an actual event, you may not want to add or change the details in your letter. However, knowing what kind of details are important to an argument and what kind aren't will help you when you take essay tests.

6 Look at another classmate's letter. What details did he or she include? Do the details support the complaint or not? Are there any other details that he or she should add?

Writing the Second Draft

7 Rewrite your letter neatly using correct form. Then give it to your teacher for comments.

PART 4   # A Step Beyond

Expansion Activities

1   Exchange letters with another student. Pretend you are the person who received the letter and decide what you will do about the complaint. Either write a reply to the letter or pretend to call the person who wrote the letter on the phone and discuss your decision.

2   Write a formal letter complaining about a problem at your school. It might be the courses the school offers, the cafeteria food, the lack of parking spaces, or anything else. Before you write your letter, find out the correct name and title of the person your letter should go to. For example, you might write to the cafeteria manager about a problem with the food. Share your letter with your classmates.

Journal Writing

3   In your journal, make two columns with these headings at the top:

What I Like about My Life Now

What I Don't Like about My Life Now

Quickly make a list of all the things you like and don't like. Then write an informal "complaint" about one of the things you don't like and what you think you can do about it.

4   Write in your journal about the most important thing(s) you have learned about writing in English since you started this course.

What Do You Think?

Analyzing Information Supporting a Complaint

In small groups, read a few of your classmates' letters of complaint. Analyze the information your classmates provided in support of their complaints. For example, consider

■   The time period between the purchase and problem

■   The claims of advertisements for the product

■   Supporting documents such as receipts and names of people

Is the information about the complaint clear and simple? Does the writer suggest a solution? Is the writer polite?

Imagine that your group works for the company or store receiving the complaint letters. What are you going to do about each complaint? Why?

Video Activities: Spoiled Kids

Before You Watch.   Discuss these questions in a group.

When you were a child:
1. How often did you receive gifts from your parents and relatives?
2. Was it hard for your parents to say "no" to you?
3. Did you have to work in the house?
4. Did you receive money from your parents?

Watch.   Write answers to these questions.

1. What are some of the toys and things that Bret (the boy) and Jessica (the girl) have in their rooms? _____

2. How did Bret and Jessica get their things? _____

3. What is Jane Annunziata's profession? _____

4. Why do some American parents give their children so much?

    _____

Watch Again.   Match the opinions on the left with the speakers on the right.

Opinion

1. _____ It's OK to have a lot of things if you appreciate what you have.
2. _____ People have a lot of money and they love their children, so they buy them toys.
3. _____ If parents have only one child, it's easy to give that child too much.
4. _____ Children who always get everything they want may have problems with their friends.
5. _____ It's easier to say yes to children than to say no.
6. _____ What children really want is time with their parents, not just a lot of stuff.

Speaker

a. Psychologist
b. Jessica's mother
c. Bret
d. Toy store owner
e. _____
f. _____

After You Watch.   In the video, Jessica's mother says, "We all want to be loved and accepted, and it's much easier to say yes than to say no."
    With a partner, write a skit (a short play) in which a teenager wants something from his or her parent and the parent says no. After you finish, read your skit for the class.

Appendix 1

Spelling Rules for Adding Endings

Endings That Begin with Vowels (*-ed, -ing, -er, -est*)

1. For words ending in a silent *e*, drop the *e* and add the ending.

   like → lik**ed**   make → mak**ing**   safe → saf**er**   fine → fin**est**

2. For one-syllable words ending in a single vowel and a single consonant, double the final consonant.

   bat → bat**ted**   run → run**ning**   fat → fat**ter**   hot → hot**test**

3. Don't double the final consonant when the word has two final consonants or two vowels before a final consonant.

   pick → pick**ed**   sing → sing**ing**   clean → clean**er**   cool → cool**est**

4. For words of two or more syllables that end in a single vowel and a single consonant, double the final consonant if the word is accented on the final syllable.

   refér → refer**red**   begín → begin**ning**

5. For words of two or more syllables that end in a single vowel and a single consonant, make no change if the word isn't accented on the final syllable.

   trável → travel**ed**   fócus → focus**ed**

6. For words ending in a consonant and *y*, change the *y* to *i* and add the ending unless the ending begins with *i*.

   stud**y** → stud**ied**   dirty → dirt**ier**   sunny → sunn**iest**

   stud**y** → stud**ying**   hurry → hurr**ying**

7. For words ending in a vowel and *y*, make no change before adding the ending.

   pla**y** → play**ed**   stay → stay**ing**

Endings That Begin with Consonants (*-ly, -ment*)

1. For words ending in a silent *e*, make no change when adding endings that begin with consonants.

   fine → fine**ly**   state → state**ment**

2. For words ending in a consonant and *y*, change the *y* to *i* before adding the ending.

   hap**py** → happ**ily**   merry → merr**iment**

Adding a Final *s* to Nouns and Verbs

1. Generally, add the *s* without making changes.

    sit → sit**s**   dance → dance**s**   play → play**s**   book → book**s**

2. If a word ends in a consonant and *y*, change the *y* to *i* and add *es*.
    marry → mar**ries**   study → stud**ies**   cherry → cher**ries**

3. If a word ends in *ch, s, sh, x,* or *z,* add *es*.
    chur**ch** → churche**s**   cash → cashe**s**   fizz → fizz**es**

    boss → bosse**s**   mix → mix**es**

4. For words ending in *o*, sometimes add *es* and sometimes add *s.*
    tomat**o** → tomato**es**   potat**o** → potato**es**

    pian**o** → piano**s**   radi**o** → radio**s**

5. For words ending in *f* or *fe,* generally drop the *f* or *fe* and add *ves.*
    knife → kni**ves**   wife → wi**ves**   life → li**ves**   loaf → loa**ves**

    Exceptions: sa**fe** → sa**fes**   puff → puff**s**   roof → roof**s**

Appendix 2

Capitalization Rules
First Words

1. Capitalize the first word of every sentence.
    They live in Rome. **W**ho is it?

2. Capitalize the first word of a quotation.
    He said, "**M**y name is Paul." Jenny asked, "**W**hen is the party?"

Personal Names

1. Capitalize the names of people including initials and titles of address.
    Mrs. **J**ones   **M**ohandas **G**andhi   **J**ohn **F. K**ennedy

2. Capitalize family words if they appear alone or followed by a name.
    Let's go, **D**ad.   Where's **G**randma?   She's at **A**unt **L**ucy's.

3. Don't capitalize family words with a possessive pronoun or article.
    my **u**ncle   her **m**other   our **g**randparents   an **a**unt

4. Capitalize the pronoun *I.*
    I have a book.   She's bigger than **I** am.

5. Capitalize names of God.

God   **Allah**   **Jesus Christ**

6. Capitalize the names of nationalities, races, peoples, and religions.

Japanese   **Arab**   **Asian**   **Chicano**   **Muslim**

7. Generally, don't capitalize occupations.

I am a **s**ecretary.   She wants to be a **l**awyer.

Place Names

1. Capitalize the names of countries, states, provinces, and cities.

Mexico   **New York**   **Ontario**   **Tokyo**

2. Capitalize the names of oceans, lakes, rivers, islands, and mountains.

the **A**tlantic **O**cean   **L**ake **C**omo   the **A**mazon   **B**elle **I**sle   **M**t. **E**verest

3. Capitalize the names of geographical areas.

the **S**outh   the **E**ast **C**oast   **A**sia   **A**ntarctica

4. Don't capitalize directions if they aren't names of geographical areas.

He lives **e**ast of Toronto.   They traveled **s**outhwest.

5. Capitalize names of schools, parks, buildings, and streets.

the **U**niversity of **G**eorgia   **C**entral **P**ark   the **S**ears **B**uilding   **O**xford **R**oad

Time Words

1. Capitalize names of days and months.

Monday   **F**riday   **J**anuary   **M**arch

2. Capitalize names of holidays and historical events.

Christmas   **N**ew **Y**ear's **D**ay   **I**ndependence **D**ay   **W**orld **W**ar II

3. Don't capitalize names of seasons.

spring   **s**ummer   **f**all   **w**inter

Titles

1. Capitalize the first word and all important words of titles of books, magazines, newspapers, and articles.

Interactions   *Newsweek*   *The New York Times*   "**R**ock **M**usic **T**oday"

2. Capitalize the first word and all important words of names of movies, plays, radio programs, and television programs.

The African Queen   *The Tempest*   "**N**ews **R**oundup"   "**F**ame"

3. Don't capitalize articles (*a, an, the*), conjunctions (*but, and, or*), and short prepositions (*of, with, in, on, for*) unless they are the first word of a title.

The Life of Thomas Edison   *War and Peace*   *Death of a Salesman*

Names of Organizations

1. Capitalize the names of organizations, government groups, and businesses.

   International Student Association   the **Senate**   **Gestetner**

2. Capitalize trade names, but do not capitalize the names of the product.
   IBM computer   **Toyota** hatchback   **Kellogg's** cereal

Other

1. Capitalize the names of languages

   Spanish   **Thai**   **French**   **Japanese**

2. Don't capitalize school subjects unless they are the names of languages or are followed by a number.
   geometry   music   **English**   **Arabic**   **Biology** 306

Appendix 3

Punctuation Rules

Period

1. Use a period after a statement or command.

   We are studying English.   Open your books to Chapter 3.

2. Use a period after most abbreviations.
   Mr.   Ms.   Dr.   Ave.   etc.   U.S.

   Exceptions: UN   NATO   IBM   AIDS

3. Use a period after initials.
   H. G. Wells   Dr. H. R. Hammond

Question Mark

1. Use a question mark after (not before) questions.

   Where are you going?   Is he here yet?

2. In a direct quotation, the question mark goes before the quotation marks.
   He asked, "What's your name?"

Exclamation Point

Use an exclamation point after exclamatory sentences or phrases.

I won the lottery!   Be quiet!   Wow!

Comma

1. Use a comma before a conjunction (*and, or, so, but*) that separates two independent clauses.

   She wanted to go to work, so she decided to take an English course.
   He wasn't happy in that apartment, but he didn't have the money to move.

2. Don't use a comma before a conjunction that separates two phrases that aren't complete sentences.

   She worked in the library and studied at night.
   Do you want to go to a movie or stay home?

3. Use a comma before an introductory clause or phrase (generally if it is five or more words long).

   After a beautiful wedding ceremony, they had a reception
   in her mother's home.
   If you want to write well, you should practice writing almost every night.

4. Use a comma to separate interrupting expressions from the rest of a sentence.

   Do you know, by the way, what time dinner is?
   Many of the students, I found out, stayed on campus during the summer.

5. Use a comma after transitional expressions.

   In addition, he stole all her jewelry.
   However, he left the TV.

   Common transitional expressions are:

therefore	in addition	in fact	on the other hand
consequently	moreover	similarly	for example
for this reason	furthermore	however	for instance
also	besides	nevertheless	

6. Use a comma to separate names of people in direct address from the rest of a sentence.

   Jane, have you seen Paul?
   We aren't sure, Mrs. Shapiro, where he is.

7. Use a comma after *yes* and *no* in answers.

   Yes, he was here a minute ago.
   No, I haven't.

8. Use a comma to separate items in a series.

   We have coffee, tea, and milk.
   He looked in the refrigerator, on the shelves, and in the cupboard.

9. Use a comma to separate an appositive from the rest of a sentence.

   Mrs. Sampson, his English teacher, gave him a good recommendation.
   Would you like to try a taco, a delicious Mexican food?

10. If a date or address has two or more parts, use a comma after each part.

    I was born on June 5, 1968.
    The house at 230 Seventh Street, Miami, Florida, is for sale.

11. Use a comma to separate contrasting information from the rest of the sentence.

It wasn't Maria, but Parvin, who was absent.
Bring your writing book, not your reading book.

12. Use a comma to separate quotations from the rest of a sentence.

He asked, "What are we going to do?"
"I'm working downtown," he said.

13. Use a comma to separate two or more adjectives that each modify the noun alone.

She was an intelligent, beautiful actress. (*intelligent* and *beautiful* actress)
Eat those delicious green beans. (*delicious* modifies *green beans*)

14. Use a comma to separate nonrestrictive clauses from the rest of a sentence. A nonrestrictive clause gives more information about the noun it describes, but it isn't needed to identify the noun. Clauses after proper names are nonrestrictive and require commas.

It's a Wonderful Life, which is often on television at Christmastime, is my favorite movie.
James Stewart, who plays a man thinking of killing himself, is the star of *It's a Wonderful Life*.

Quotation Marks

1. Use quotation marks at the beginning and end of exact quotations. Other punctuation marks go before the end quotation marks.

He said, "I'm going to Montreal."
"How are you?" he asked.

2. Use quotation marks before and after titles of stories, articles, songs, and television programs. Periods and commas go before the final quotation marks, while question marks and exclamation points normally go after them.

Do you like to watch "Dallas" on television?
My favorite song is "Let It Be."
Do you like the story "Gift of the Magi"?

Apostrophes

1. Use apostrophes in contractions.

don't   it's   we've   they're

2. Use an apostrophe to make possessive nouns.

Singular: Jerry's   my boss's
Plural: the children's   the Smiths'

Underlining

Underline the titles of books, magazines, newspapers, plays, and movies.

I am reading <u>One Hundred Years of Solitude</u>.

Did you like the movie <u>The Wizard of Oz</u>?

Chapter 1

Feedback Sheet

Student Name _____ Date _____

Personal Reaction

_____

_____

_____

_____

Chapter Checklist	**Good**	**Needs Work**
1. Content		
a. Is the information about your partner interesting?	❑	❑
b. Is it complete?	❑	❑
c. Is it correct?	❑	❑
2. Organization		
a. Are all the sentences about one topic?	❑	❑
b. Is the order of the sentences easy to follow?	❑	❑
3. Cohesion and Style		
a. Are your sentences clear and simple?	❑	❑
b. Are they easy to understand?	❑	❑
c. Can you connect any sentences?	❑	❑
4. Grammar		
a. Is the grammar correct?	❑	❑
b. Are your verbs correct?	❑	❑
Remember that third-person singular verbs end with *-s* in the present tense. Also check that your negative verbs are correct.		
c. Are singular and plural nouns correct?	❑	❑
d. Is the word order in your sentences correct?	❑	❑
5. Form		
a. Is your punctuation correct?	❑	❑
b. Is your spelling correct?	❑	❑
c. Is your paragraph and sentence form correct?	❑	❑

Other Comments

_____

_____

_____

_____

189

Chapter 2

Feedback Sheet

Student Name _____ Date _____

Personal Reaction

_____

_____

_____

_____

Chapter Checklist	**Good**	**Needs Work**
1. Content		
a. Are there interesting adjectives in the paragraph?	❑	❑
b. Do the adjectives describe the picture well?	❑	❑
2. Organization		
a. Does the paragraph move from general to specific?	❑	❑
b. Do you need to change the order of the sentences?	❑	❑
3. Cohesion and Style		
a. Can you connect any sentences?	❑	❑
b. Are the pronouns correct?	❑	❑
c. Are the adjectives in the correct place?	❑	❑
d. Are the prepositional phrases appropriate?	❑	❑
4. Grammar		
a. Are the verb forms correct? Is there an -s ending on all third-person singular verbs? (The use of the -s ending on verbs is subject-verb agreement.)	❑	❑
b. Is the use of *a/an* and the correct?	❑	❑
5. Form		
a. Does the paragraph follow the rules for correct form? If you aren't sure, look back at the rules for the form of a paragraph on page 12.	❑	❑
b. Are the present participles correct?		

Other Comments

_____

_____

_____

_____

Chapter 3

Feedback Sheet

Student Name _____ Date _____

Personal Reaction

_____
_____
_____
_____

Chapter Checklist	Good	Needs Work
1. Content		
a. Is the paragraph interesting?	❑	❑
b. Is the information clear?	❑	❑
2. Organization		
a. Does the topic sentence give the main idea of the paragraph?	❑	❑
Is it a complete sentence?	❑	❑
b. Are all the sentences about the holiday?	❑	❑
c. Are the sentences in logical order?	❑	❑
3. Cohesion and Style		
a. Can you connect any sentences with *and, so*, or *but*?	❑	❑
b. Are the appositives correct?	❑	❑
c. Does *such as* introduce examples?	❑	❑
4. Grammar		
a. Are the present tense verbs correct?	❑	❑
b. Are the count and noncount nouns correct?	❑	❑
5. Form		
a. Is the paragraph form (indentation, capitalization, and punctuation) correct?	❑	❑
b. Is the spelling of words with *-s* endings correct?	❑	❑
c. Is the use of commas with appositives correct?	❑	❑

Other Comments

_____
_____
_____
_____

193

Chapter 4

Student Name _____ Date _____

Personal Reaction

_____

_____

_____

_____

Chapter Checklist	**Good**	**Needs Work**
1. Content		
a. Are the activities interesting?	❏	❏
b. Are the directions clear?	❏	❏
2. Organization		
Is each paragraph about a different topic?	❏	❏
3. Cohesion and Style		
a. Are the propositions correct?	❏	❏
b. Is the use of *there* and *it* correct?	❏	❏
4. Grammar		
Are the verb forms correct?	❏	❏
5. Form		
a. Is the date correct?	❏	❏
b. Is the salutation correct?	❏	❏
c. Do the paragraphs begin with an indentation?	❏	❏
d. Is the closing in the right place?	❏	❏

Other Comments

_____

_____

_____

_____

Chapter 5

Feedback Sheet

Student Name _____ Date _____

Personal Reaction

_____

_____

_____

_____

Chapter Checklist	Good	Needs Work
1. Content		
a. Is the information interesting?	❏	❏
b. Is the information important?	❏	❏
c. Is there an interesting title?	❏	❏
2. Organization		
a. Does the topic sentence give the main idea of the paragraph?	❏	❏
b. Are all the sentences about one topic?	❏	❏
c. Should you change the order of any of the sentences?	❏	❏
3. Cohesion and Style		
Did you combine sentences with time words and *and, but, so,* and *because?*	❏	❏
4. Grammar		
a. Are your nouns, pronouns, and articles correct?	❏	❏
b. Did you use good sentence structure (no sentence fragments)?	❏	❏
c. Did you use the correct past tense verbs?	❏	❏
5. Form		
a. Did you use the correct paragraph form?	❏	❏
b. Did you capitalize the words in the title correctly?	❏	❏
c. Did you use correct punctuation when you combined sentences?	❏	❏

Other Comments

_____

_____

_____

_____

Chapter 6

Student Name _____   Date _____

Personal Reaction

_____

_____

_____

_____

Chapter Checklist	**Good**	**Needs Work**
1. Content		
a. Is the story clear?	❏	❏
b. Is all the information important?	❏	❏
2. Organization		
a. Did you use time words where necessary?	❏	❏
b. Did you add a title?	❏	❏
c. Should you change the order of any of the sentences?	❏	❏
3. Cohesion and Style		
a. Did you vary the time words and expressions?	❏	❏
b. Did you include enough description?	❏	❏
c. Did you use quotations?	❏	❏
4. Grammar		
a. Did you use the correct forms of the past tense?	❏	❏
b. Did you use the correct forms of the present continuous tense?	❏	❏
c. Did you use good sentence structure (no fragments)?	❏	❏
5. Form		
a. Did you use commas correctly?	❏	❏
b. Did you use quotation marks correctly?	❏	❏

Other Comments

_____

_____

_____

_____

Chapter 7

Feedback Sheet

Student Name _____ Date _____

Personal Reaction

_____
_____
_____
_____

Chapter Checklist	Good	Needs Work
1. Content		
a. Is the information interesting?	❏	❏
b. Are there purposes and examples in the paragraph?	❏	❏
2. Organization		
a. Does the topic sentence give the main idea of the paragraph?	❏	❏
b. Are all the sentences about the topic of the paragraph?	❏	❏
3. Cohesion and Style		
a. Did you use relative clauses correctly?	❏	❏
b. Did you use transitional words and phrases correctly?	❏	❏
c. Did you use quotations?	❏	❏
4. Grammar		
a. Did you use correct noun forms?	❏	❏
b. Did you use correct verb forms?	❏	❏
c. Did you use good sentence structure (no fragments)?	❏	❏
5. Form		
Are there commas after transitional words and after dependent clauses?	❏	❏

Other Comments

_____
_____
_____
_____

Chapter 8

Feedback Sheet

Student Name _____ Date _____

Personal Reaction

_____

_____

_____

_____

Chapter Checklist	Good	Needs Work
1. Content		
a. Is the title interesting?	❏	❏
b. Would other people want to see the movie because of your summary?	❏	❏
c. Did you present the problem and the events leading to the solution?	❏	❏
d. Does your summary include the type of movie, when and where the movie takes place, and the main characters?	❏	❏
2. Organization		
a. Is all the information in the paragraph important?	❏	❏
b. Does the topic sentence give a general idea of what kind of movie you're writing about?	❏	❏
3. Cohesion and Style		
a. Did you combine sentences to show the relationship between events?	❏	❏
b. Did you use appositives correctly?	❏	❏
c. Did you use adjectives to describe the characters and the movie?	❏	❏
d. Did you use the historical present tense?	❏	❏
4. Grammar		
a. Are the present tense verbs correct?	❏	❏
b. Are the count and noncount nouns correct?	❏	❏
c. Did you combine sentences correctly?	❏	❏
5. Form		
a. Did you underline the title of the movie?	❏	❏
b. Did you use commas with appositives and adjectives correctly?	❏	❏

Other Comments

_____

_____

_____

_____

203

Chapter 9

Feedback Sheet

Student Name _____ Date _____

Personal Reaction

_____

_____

_____

_____

Chapter Checklist	Good	Needs Work
1. Content		
a. Is the information interesting?	❏	❏
b. Is all the information in the paragraph important?	❏	❏
2. Organization		
a. Does the topic sentence give the main idea of the paragraph?	❏	❏
b. Are the sentences well organized?	❏	❏
c. Does the paragraph have a good concluding sentence?	❏	❏
3. Cohesion and Style		
a. Did you use transitional expressions correctly?	❏	❏
b. Did you use *so . . . that* correctly?	❏	❏
c. Did you use long forms rather than contractions as appropriate?	❏	❏
4. Grammar		
Did you use correct verb form?	❏	❏
5. Form		
a. Did you use commas correctly?	❏	❏
b. Did you spell the verb forms correctly?	❏	❏
c. Did you use correct capitalization?	❏	❏

Other Comments

_____

_____

_____

_____

Chapter 10

Student Name _____ Date _____

Personal Reaction

_____

_____

_____

_____

Chapter Checklist	Good	Needs Work
1. Content		
a. Is the information interesting?	❏	❏
b. Is there enough information?	❏	❏
2. Organization		
a. Did you list the holidays from most important to least important?	❏	❏
b. Did you give the same type of information about each holiday?	❏	❏
3. Cohesion and Style		
a. Did you use expressions such as *in addition to, besides, another, the first (second, etc.)*?	❏	❏
b. Did you use quantifiers correctly?	❏	❏
c. Did you use pronouns and pronominal expressions appropriately?	❏	❏
d. Did you use relative clauses correctly?	❏	❏
4. Grammar		
a. Are the verb forms correct?	❏	❏
b. Are there any sentence fragments?	❏	❏
5. Form		
Do the relative clauses have commas where necessary?	❏	❏

Other Comments

_____

_____

_____

_____

Chapter 11

Feedback Sheet

Student Name _____ Date _____

Personal Reaction

_____
_____
_____
_____

Chapter Checklist	Good	Needs Work
1. Content		
a. Does the message express your opinion strongly without personal attacks?	❏	❏
b. Have you given reasons and examples to support your opinion?	❏	❏
2. Organization		
a. Are all your sentences on the topic on the discussion group?	❏	❏
b. Does your message contain a sentence or two that gives the main idea of your message?	❏	❏
c. Does your topic line give the main idea of your message and make people want to read it?	❏	❏
3. Cohesion and Style		
a. Does your message use pronouns and synonyms to unify your writing?	❏	❏
b. Have you used polite phrases to give opinions and suggestions?	❏	❏
4. Grammar		
a. Are your verbs correct?	❏	❏
b. Have you used correct grammatical forms to give opinions and suggestions?	❏	❏
5. Form		
a. Have you avoided writing in all capitals?	❏	❏
b. Have you capitalized the important words in your topic line correctly?	❏	❏
c. Have you written a signature under your message with your name and electronic address?	❏	❏

Other Comments

_____
_____
_____
_____

Chapter 12

Feedback Sheet

Student Name _____   Date _____

Personal Reaction

_____

_____

_____

_____

Chapter Checklist	**Good**	**Needs Work**
1. Content Did you explain the problem clearly?	❏	❏
2. Organization a. Did you include all the necessary details?	❏	❏
b. Did you include any unnecessary details?	❏	❏
3. Cohesion and Style a. Did you use formal language?	❏	❏
b. Did you use polite language?	❏	❏
4. Grammar a. Did you use correct verb forms?	❏	❏
b. Did you use past participles as adjectives correctly?	❏	❏
5. Form Did you use the correct business letter format, with a date, inside address, salutation, and closing?	❏	❏

Other Comments

_____

_____

_____

_____